NX Expressions for Smarties

Covers all current versions in 38 exercises

Stephen M. Samuel, PE

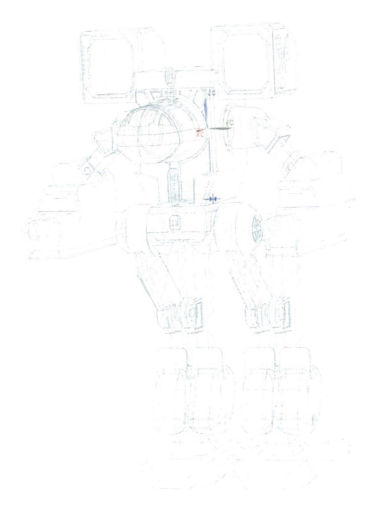

DESIGN VISIONARIES
Superior Vision Yields Optimal Products

ISBN: 978-1-935951032

—

Published by:

Design Visionaries

7034 Calcaterra Drive

San Jose, CA 95120

info@designviz.com

http://designvisionaries.com

http://nxtutorials.com

Local Phone: (408) 997 6323

Fax: (408) 997 9667

Written and printed with great pride in the United States of America
Published March 2013

About the Author

Stephen M. Samuel PE, Founder and President of Design Visionaries, has over 26 years' experience in developing and using high-end CAD tools and mentoring its users. During a ten-year career at Pratt & Whitney Aircraft, he was responsible for implementing advanced CAD/CAM technology in a design/manufacturing environment. After founding Design Visionaries he has trained thousands of engineers in Unigraphics, written self-paced courses in UG/NX Advanced Modeling and Best Practices, and performed design work for numerous Fortune 500 companies. Stephen is the author of distinctive publications on NX Nastran, UGNX CAD, Sold Edge, SolidWorks, and TeamCenter Engineering PLM. Stephen holds several US patents and enjoys a life of creativity and intellectual challenge in the city of San Jose, CA. He happily shares his life with three amazing children, his best friend wife and an 81 year old powerhouse of a mother that lives in her home right next door.

Hey! What can I say? I'm a nerd who really loves to design and build stuff. I also love to share what I've learned. Hope you enjoy.

Special Thanks:

To Landon Ritchie: Thank you for the cover art, editing, file conversion, content and constant support. Thanks for being an incredibly fast learner and a friend. Thank you to all the other people who read this and made copious suggestion and criticism.

Thank you to Taylor Anderson from Siemens who helped with accuracy and content—an awesome hard core nerd. And thanks to Siemens for overall support.

Thank you to my incredibly supportive family without whom all of this would be impossible.

Special thanks to the United States of America and all those who built it and fought for it including the public schools that were instrumental in allowing me such a rich opportunity.

About this course

Welcome! This course on the expressions language in NX has been written for engineers by engineers who love this stuff. We did it knowing that you're probably very busy. That said, we've made this course very hands-on and streamlined. Most of this course is made up of exercises. You will learn a ton by performing them. The exercises get successively more difficult as the chapters progress, so we expect that if you already know a bit about expressions you can skip the beginning chapters and start somewhere in the middle.

Due to the raw power of expressions in NX this course is quite extensive. Most folks who use NX know at least a little about expressions but when you get into the detail you come to realize that the subject is vast. The expressions capability in NX is arguably the best, most powerful and easiest to use capability of its kind when compared to all the other major CAD programs. Most of the other CAD programs with a similar ability require you to order the expressions, "relations" just right, and you cannot make expressions on the fly. Also on other programs the available functions are limited and cumbersome. This course is an attempt to capture it all and provide real world examples from industry.

The examples in this course are done in inches. In most cases it doesn't matter if you do them in inches or millimeters. Every exercise has been worked through and the resulting files have been organized and posted at http://designvisionaries.com/goodies/workfiles/

The techniques captured in this course reflect years of actual experience working with some of the most aggressive Fortune 500 engineering firms. It has been our privilege and pleasure to work with the engineering community for over 20 years amassing this highly interesting knowledge and sharing it with you the NX user community. Thank you so very much.

Why a separate course in NX expressions language?

The use of NX expressions language is one of the biggest advantages to choosing NX. The subject is so vast and mastering the techniques makes such a huge difference in your ability to build high quality models quickly and efficiently, that the subject warranted its own mini course. Mastering NX expressions gives you a pervasive advantage when creating almost all features in addition to synchronous modeling, surfacing, sheet metal, drafting, machining and even NX Nastran.

Who should take this course?

This course has been written for both basic and very advanced NX users who truly want to access the full power of NX. The exercises span the entire range. Advanced users will want to begin somewhere in the middle. In the end analysis almost everyone who is doing parametric modeling will benefit.

Dedication

To the men and women who commit their lives to public service. You teach us, heal us, and protect us. You are under-appreciated heroes. Thank you so very much.

Contents

1. Introduction to Expressions

The ability to create expressions is one of the most powerful and unique tools included in NX. Expressions are the easiest way to capture design intent and engineering relations even before you've created the first actual geometric entity. Expressions are variables that are created automatically and/or manually as you create various features. They are the underlying numerical values that drive and define every parametric feature. When you create a sketch or a primitive, expressions are automatically created and are labeled sequentially by default p1, p2, p3 etc. As you continue to create your model you can re-name the expressions that are automatically created or you can create your own. You can use good descriptive names such as "thk" for thickness and "l" for length so that you or your colleagues can pick up a model after being away from it for months and instantly understand exactly what has been done. You can even use expressions to link values from one component to another.

The expressions can include every manner of mathematical operator such as sin, cos, ln, sqrt and almost anything else an engineer might want. There are hundreds of other built in functions such as beam equations, o-ring seal equations and many other engineering formulas. You can use "if - than - else" statements and string variables too. If you perform all the exercises in this short course you will know almost all there is to know about expressions language in NX.

Each section in this course will begin with an explanation of each expression language topic and will then be followed by one or more actual exercises. The exercises will have most of the button presses and menu choices detailed out and will lead you through the use of the various techniques. The end of each exercise is signified by a short note "**End of exercise**". Learning more about the expressions language will enable you to create better CAD models that will help you to be far more productive and ultimately produce better designs faster.

Exercise 1.1 Understanding the Expressions Dialog

In this exercise you will be introduced to the basic expression dialog.

First, create a new part file and open the expressions editor window in NX. You can get to it by going to **Tools -> Expression** or by using the **ctrl-E** keyboard accelerator. You should see the following window below:

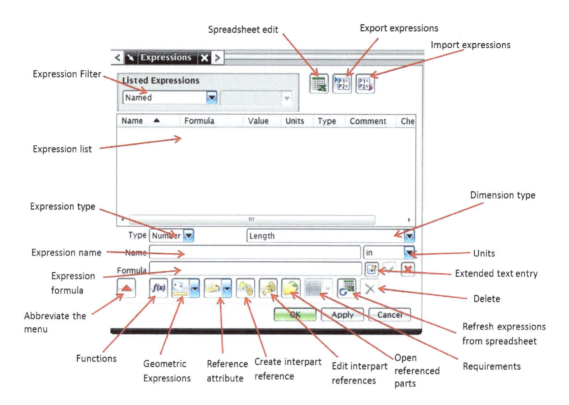

The figure above shows you what each button does. Notice that as you move your cursor over each icon, you receive a note on the screen telling you the identity of the various functions.

End of Exercise.

Exercise 1.2 Creating Expressions

In this exercise you will learn how to create expressions and use them in a sketch.

In a new part with inch units open up the expressions editor by selecting **Tools -> Expression**. Type in "**mylength**" into the name field. Notice how the cursor goes into the **Formula** field as soon as you type in "**=**".

Next enter a value of **10** into the Formula field.

Select **Apply** and the expression will be saved into the expression list.

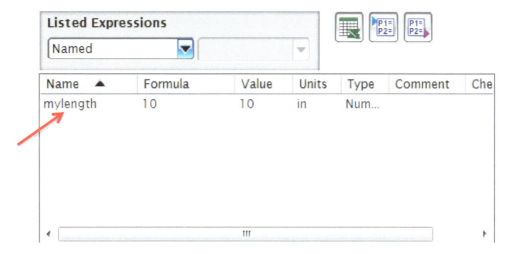

Next create another expression named **rad** with a value of 2. Follow the same steps as before. Afterwards make a rectangle sketch with a circle drawn inside.

Using the inferred dimension tool create a dimension along the side of the rectangle, then type in the **mylength** expression name and press enter.

Do the same for the diameter of the circle, type in the expression named **rad** and press enter. You should have a sketch similar to the image below.

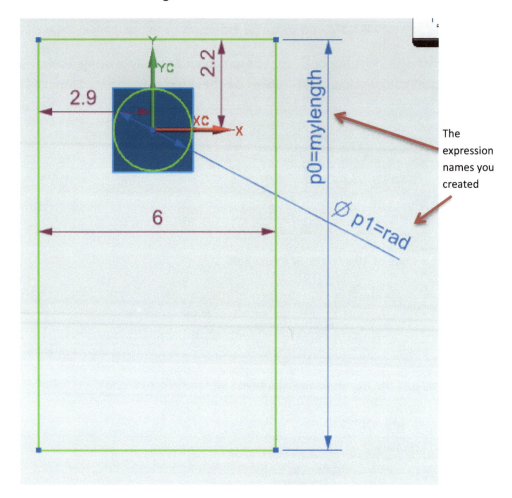

The expression names you created

Now finish the sketch and perform an extrude command on the sketch to make it about 4 inches tall.

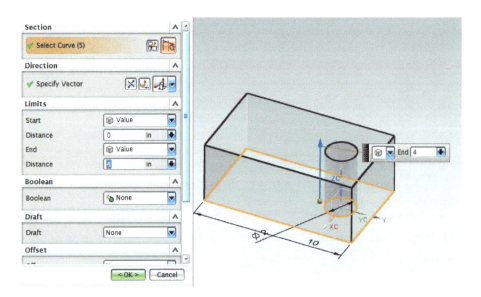

What is created is a 3D block with a hole in it. The greatest and most powerful thing about expressions is that you can now alter the shape of this geometry without having to go back into the lower levels of sketching to modify the dimensions. You can do it all from the expression editor.

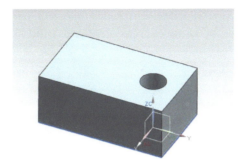

To continue open the expressions editor again and change **mylength** to **6** by clicking on the **mylength** expression in the list and changing the value in the formula window.

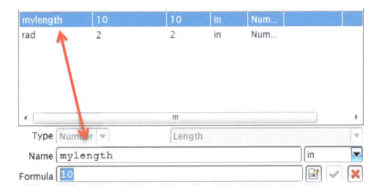

Change the value from **10** to **6** and press enter or press the little green check mark to the right of the Formula field. Then click on **rad** and change it from **2** to **3** and press enter. Now hit apply and watch as the model updates to reflect the changes you made to the expressions.

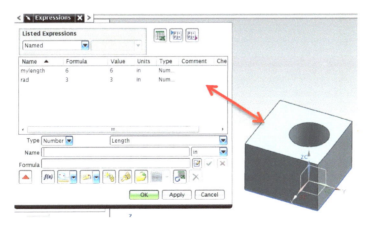

End of Exercise.

Exercise 1.3: Using and Applying Expressions

In this exercise you will learn how to apply expressions to extrusions and other features.

In a new part file, create the following expressions table: **tmid=6, tside=14** and **ttop=18.**

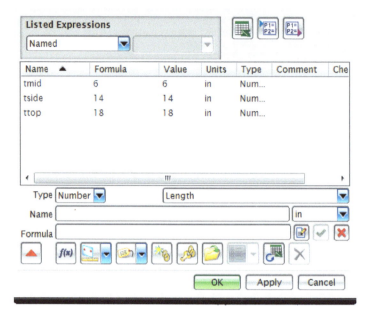

Using the expressions above create the following sketch. Don't worry that it is not fully constrained.

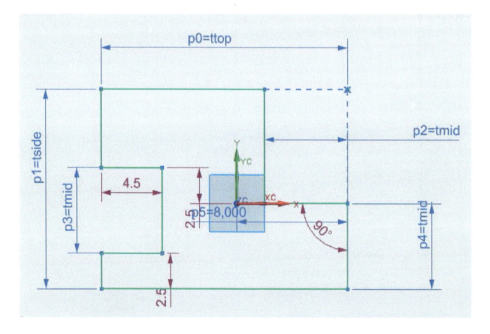

Next extrude it using the **tmid** expression as shown below; you simply enter **tmid** into the **End Distance** input field before selecting **OK.**

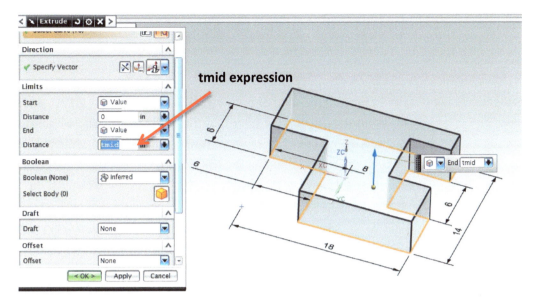

Hit **OK** to get the model below:

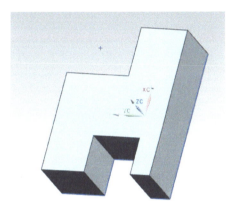

Next modify the expressions in the expression editor until you have the same model as shown below. Set **Tmid=3**.

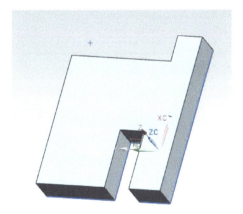

End of Exercise.

Exercise 1.4 Creating Expressions on the Fly

As you are modeling, you can create and name expressions on the fly. For example, if you are using the shell command to shell a housing, instead of entering into the shell dialog ".125" you can enter "**thk=.125**". Once you press enter, NX will remember that the shell is controlled by the expression **thk**. In essence NX simultaneously creates the variable **thk** and sets the value of the shell to the required value. This saves you the step of creating the **thk** expression beforehand. This is useful because when you create other pieces of geometry that relate to the wall thickness you can type in a relationship. For example, if you are creating injection molded geometry you will want to ensure that the ribs inside of the product are no thicker than **.65** of the nominal wall thickness to avoid sink marks. When you create the ribs you will enter in a thickness of **thk*.65** instead of the calculated value **.08125**. The beauty of using the **thk** variable instead typing in **.125** is that if and when you decide to change the nominal wall thickness, all you have to do is change the value of **thk** and the rib will automatically change to **.65** of the new thickness.

To practice these principles create a new part file and make a block in it that is 5 inches by 3 inches by 1. It should appear as the image below:

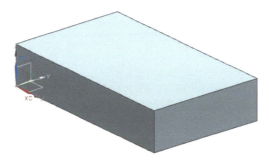

Next use the shell command selecting the bottom face and one of the side faces to remove. As you shell, enter "**thk=.125**" into the Thickness box. This will simultaneously create the **thk** variable and apply that expression to the wall thickness.

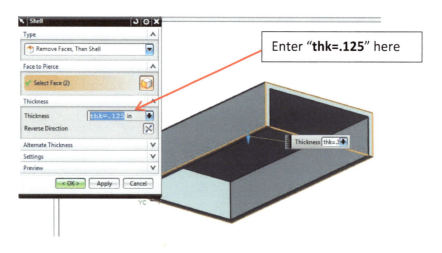

Now make a rib in the middle of the shelled solid and set the thickness of the rib equal to **.65** of the wall thickness. This can be accomplished using a sketch as shown below:

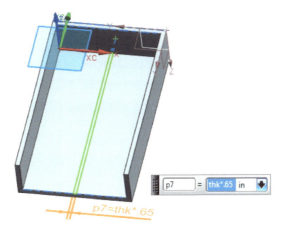

Next extrude and unite the rib to a height of .5 inches.

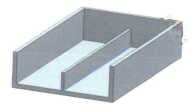

Now enter the expressions editor and change **thk** to .3. The model should change in such a way that the rib maintains its .65 relationship to the nominal wall thickness. For this exercise we are avoiding the draft that would normally be on all the walls for the sake of simplicity.

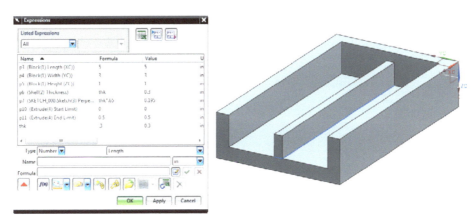

The cool thing about making expressions on the fly is that you are able to simultaneously create the expression, set the value, and apply it to an actual feature. This makes it extremely easy to capture design intent as you go through the modeling process. This means you are a lot more likely to think of the most advantageous relationships and keep track of them.

End of Exercise.

Exercise 1.5 Deleting and Renaming Expressions

During the course of creating expressions you will find it necessary to delete and rename them. When deleting an expression, you simply highlight it in the expression editor, then click the delete button — the one with the black X icon near the bottom of the dialog. The expression will not be deleted if it is in use. To demonstrate, create a 3 by 2 by 1 cube. **Insert / Design Feature / Block** and enter **3** tab **2** tab **1**. Now enter the expressions editor **Insert / Tools / Expressions, and** enter two new expressions **X=5** and **Y=3**.

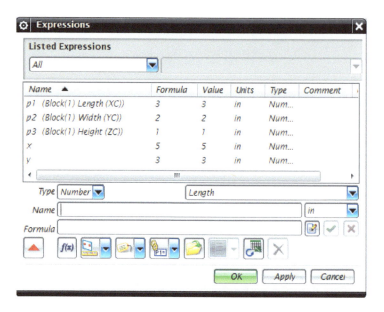

Next rename the length assigned to the **X** direction for the block by clicking on it, in this case it is **p1** and typing in "**base**".

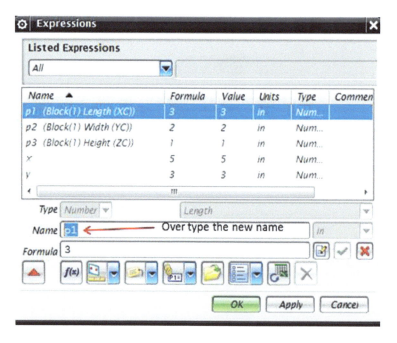

Next, attempt to delete the expression for the height of the block - in this case **p3.** Click on **p3** and notice that the delete button is not enabled.

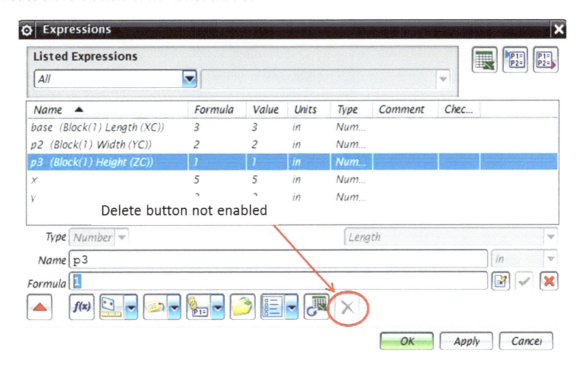

Finally delete the **X** expression that you created earlier. Highlight it and select the delete button.

End of Exercise

Exercise 1.6 Typing Completion of Expressions

NX has been programmed to save you as much time as possible and to help you be as efficient as possible. When you type certain letters into the **Formula** box, NX will bring up a menu that contains choices that are commensurate with the various commands that begin with the same letter. For example, create a new part file and bring up the expression editor. Next input **a=3**. As previously mentioned the **a** will be input into the Name box and as soon as you type "=" the 3 will go right into the **Formula** box. Since **3** does not resemble any other command no choice menu will appear. Next input **b=a.** As soon as the **a** is typed the auto complete menu will appear. The choices are **abs()**, **acosine()**, and all the other commands that begin with the letter **a**. If one of these were desired you may use the arrow keys or the mouse to select it. Upon selecting **OK** the function is loaded into the **Formula** menu. Notice how the menu disappears as soon as you hit the space bar. This is because there is no other menu choice that begins with "**a space**".

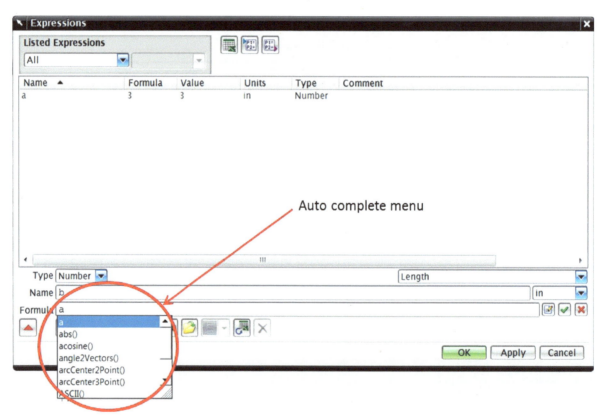

End of exercise

2. Expression Dimensions and Units

This section covers the different types of dimensions and units available in expressions as well as how they need to be used in order to achieve complex modeling tasks. By default the expressions that are typed into the expression editor are numbers that have the dimension of length and the units of whatever template you choose when you started NX. However, as you advance you may need to create variables with dimensions of **force**, **area**, or **volume**. The choice is based on your need and is selected by clicking the small down arrow to the right of the box marked **Length**.

As seen in the expression editor, there are various dimensions for the various expression types:

As shown in the example sketch below you may utilize length and or angle dimensions.

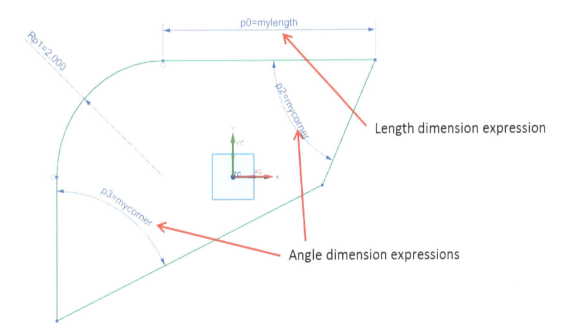

Length dimension expression

Angle dimension expressions

Some times the dimensions and units can be a little confusing. For example, if you are trying to create an expression that calculates the area of a reactangular plane, you may simply try to put in **a=p1*p2**. Upon doing so, NX will give you an error because when you multiply two lengths together it becomes an area and by default **a** will be a length variable. To rectify the problem go to the dimension box and choose dimensions of either area or constant. Then you will be able to type **a=p1*p2** and it will work.

One of the cool things about NX expressions is they have automatic units conversion. For example, if you want to know how many square meters is equivalent to **35** square feet simply create an expression "**a**" with the units of square feet and assign it a value of **35**. Then make another expression called "**b**" with units of meters squared and set **b** equal to **a**. The result of **3.2516** will appear in the **Value** column of the expression editor.

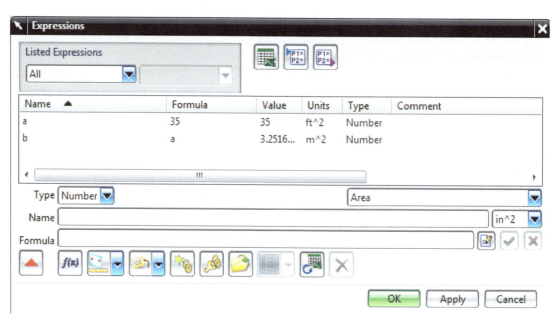

Exercise 2.1: Using Dimensions and Units

In this exercise you obtain hands-on practice with dimensions and units in the expressions editor. To proceed, open a new inch part file and name it "**volume block**". Next create a block solid that is 10 by 5 by 2 inches. Theoretically the volume of such a block is 10 times 5 times 2 or 100 cubic inches.

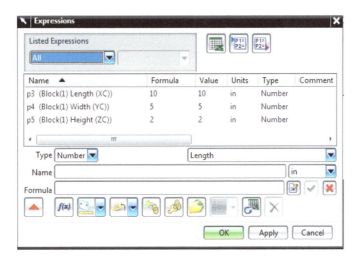

Next, open up the expressions editor so you can see the expressions that have been created. Notice all the units are listed as inch.

Next try to create a volume expression **Enter V=p3*p4*p5.** You will receive the following error message:

Now click on the down arrow to the right of the dimensions box and choose the **Volume** type switch shown below:

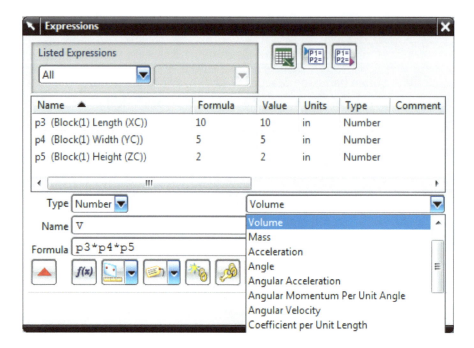

Once you make the change to **Volume** the expression will work. Take a look at how the units are listed in the expression editor. You will see the units of cubic inches.

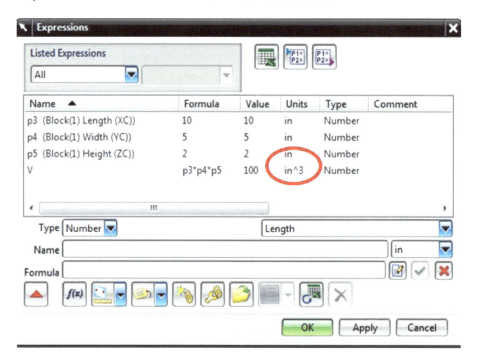

End of Exercise.

Exercise 2.2: Using the Angle Dimension

For this exercise create a new inch part file, the name does not matter. Now open the expressions editor and set the dimension to **angle**:

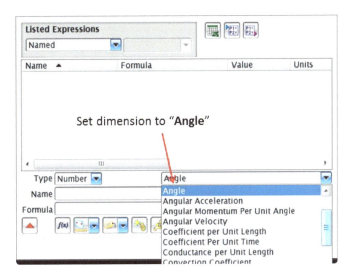

Next, create the following expressions as angles.

arms	130	130	degrees	Num...
legs	150	150	degrees	Num...

Then create the following sketch. The lengths of the arms etc. are not that important but you should make sure you have the angles on the arms constrained and dimensioned as shown below:

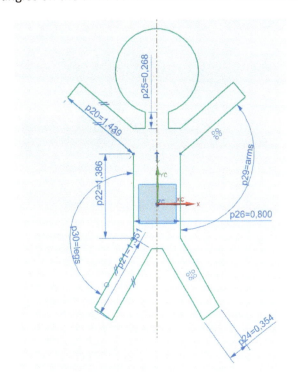

Finish the sketch, extrude the sketch, then create an edge blend around the model's edges as shown below.

Now using expressions make him exercise by changing the angle.

End of Exercise

Exercise 2.3: Using the Expressions Editor for Units Conversion

In this exercise you will use the awesome power of the expressions editor to convert a number of lengths in a pool to the number of miles a swimmer achieves in the morning swim. Jane works out in a 50 meter pool and she does her standard workout of 60 lengths. She wonders how far she's gone in miles. She just happens to have NX running on her waterproof lap top —pool side. To redo her calculations create a new inch based part file. Create an expression called "**number_of_laps**" and make it a constant and set it equal to **60**.

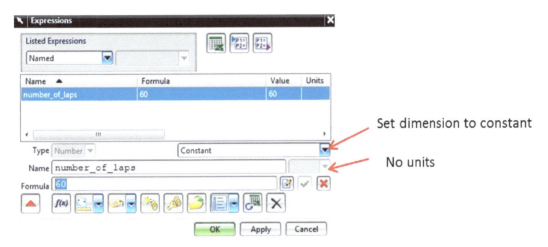

Next make an expression called "**lap_length**". Give it dimensions of **length** and units of **meters**.

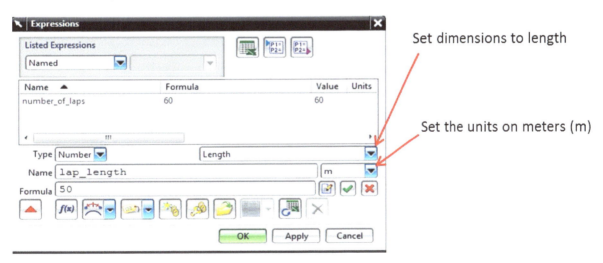

Finally make an expression called "**swim_miles**". Set it equal to "**number_of_laps * Lap_length**". Give it dimensions of length and units of miles (**mi**).

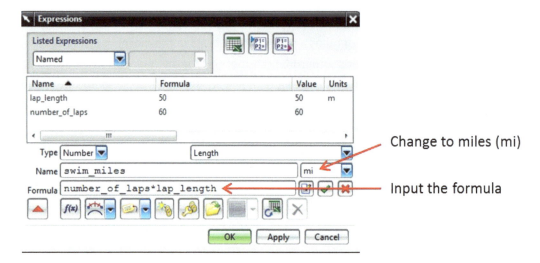

Change to miles (mi)

Input the formula

Upon selecting **OK** you can see that Jane swims about 1.9 miles. Pretty good Jane!

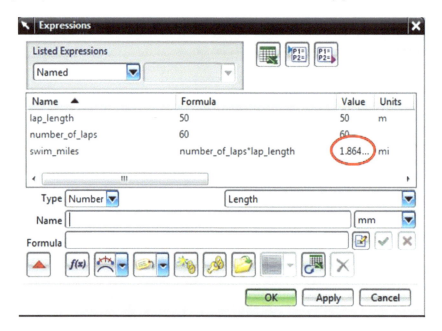

End of Exercise

3. Commenting Expressions

One of the difficult aspects of using advanced parametric CAD is trying to remember all the design intent that may go into a model, especially after time not having seen it. In some sense a complex CAD model is a program in and of itself that produces geometry. Things can get very confusing. Commenting expressions helps you to understand how a model is created and what's important about a model at a glance without having to navigate through the Part Navigator tree. Comments can be incredibly useful to someone who is using a model that they did not build so they have no recollection of what was done and why.

There are two main ways of commenting your expression; you can **double click** in the comment field to the right of any expression in the expressions editor, or you can type two forward slashes after any input value followed by the desired comment. For example, a face plate for an electrical outlet is created but the designer wants to make sure that the shape is always compliant with the golden rectangle ratio "1.618". The width of the face plate will be set to 2.95 inches and the length will be 2.95 times 1.618 or 4.77. This relationship is important to the designer but the designer knows that someone else who is using the model may not understand the 1.618 ratio. A comment is placed in the comment field.

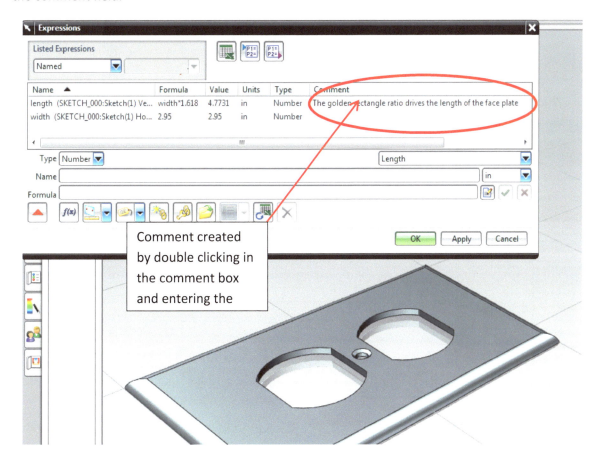

As shown above the comment is displayed in the comment field when the expression editor is being used.

Exercise 3.1: Commenting Expressions in Four Different Ways

In this exercise you will learn the four ways of commenting your expressions. First open a new part file. Click on **Tools / Expression** and bring up the expressions editor. Enter the first expression. "**Length = 5// this is the length of the butter dish**" Note: The quotes in the last sentence are just to differentiate what you're supposed to type in. Do not type them in. Also, when you type the expression in, as soon as you type in the equal sign, the cursor will automatically go to the formula box.

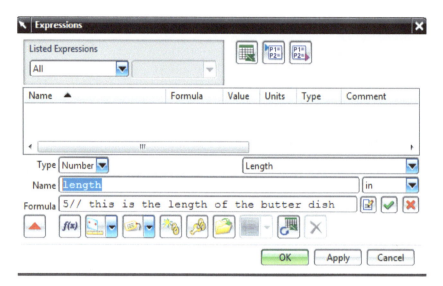

When you select **Enter**, the expression will be created with the comment automatically added into the comment column.

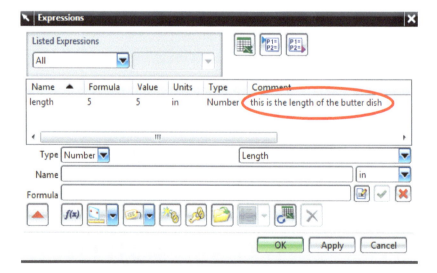

Next create another expression for the height of the butter dish. Enter **height = 1.5** and select **Enter**.

Now double click in the comment field next to the height expression. Enter a comment into the box that appears. Enter "**this is the height of the butter dish**".

The next way to create an expression is to highlight the expression in the expressions list and right click. This will create a popup menu and you can select "**Edit Comment**".

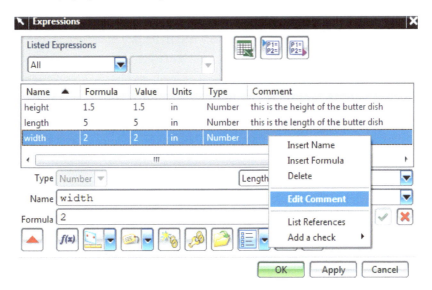

As soon as you click on **Edit Comment** you will get the same little box. Enter "**width of dish**".

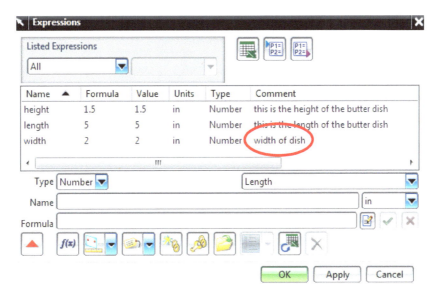

Next create a sketch that will be extruded. The sketch is dimensioned with the **length** and **width** as shown below:

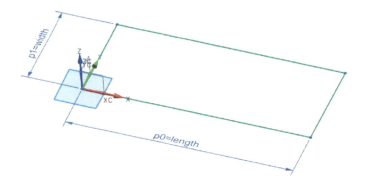

When you extrude the sketch enter **height** into the end distance box and in the draft angle box enter "**draft=12//this is the draft of the dish**". You will have simultaneously created the expression "**draft**", set the draft angle at **12**, created the comment, and created the dish solid. Pretty cool!

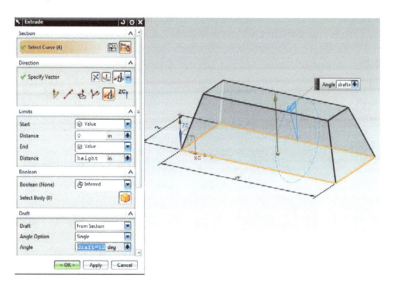

To finish off, just for giggles, take one last look at the expression editor. Verify that you created the comment "**this is the draft of the dish**", and then blend the corners with a suitable radius and shell.

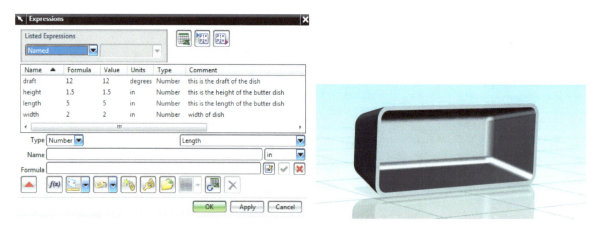

End of Exercise

4. Measurement Expressions

The measurement expression is an incredibly useful expression command. It is essentially a way of capturing data such as surface area, volume, radius of gyration, etc. and using it in an expression that you can drive other geometric entities with. For example, if you create a bent up tube out of multiple arcs, splines and lines and you join them all together, you can assign a "**measure length**" measurement expression to them and you can in turn use that value to drive a straight tube. This way you can have a bent tube component part file with a straight tube represented on the drawing that shows the correct length.

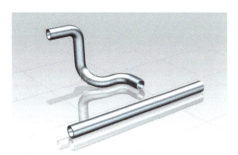

In order to access the measurement expressions one has only to access the expressions editor and click on the extended menu shown below. You have your choice of length, distance, angle, bodies and surface area. Other measurement commands are also available in the **Analysis** pull down menu.

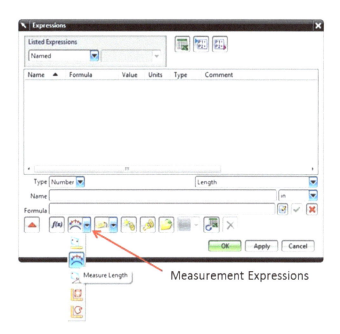

There is another way to create a measurement expression. You may access the **Analysis** menu and use many of the Analysis sub commands. When you edit the settings and choose "**Associative**", the results become measurement expressions.

Exercise 4.1: Measurement Expression – Measure Bodies

Imagine you are in charge of a machine that spits out gold ingots. The only problem is you have to know exactly how much each one weighs and costs. You are given the length, width, height, draft angle, and edge blends. The density and price per ounce of gold are found on-line. All you have to do is to create a CAD model with a measurement expression that tells you the weight and create one more expression that calculates the total cost.

First create a bunch of standard expressions as shown below. Make sure the "**Draft_angle**" expression is set to the dimension of **angle** and the units of **degrees**.

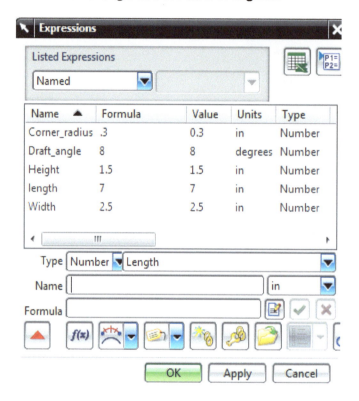

Next use the Length, Width and Height dimensions to create a block.

Then use the **Draft_angle**, and **Corner_radius** expressions to complete it. If you want to get fancy you can use the **Text** command to extrude lettering on the top.

Next apply the correct density to the model. The internet says the density of gold is 19.32 grams per cm^3. That is .698 lbs. per inch^3. If you do not have Gold as an option in your materials list you can edit the density of the solid by selecting **Edit / Feature / Solid Density**.

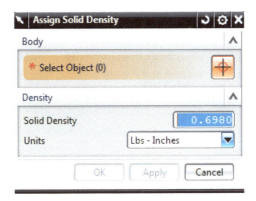

Enter in .698 and click on the solid body. Select OK.

Next access the expression editor and select the **Measure Bodies** option from the measurement pull-down menu. Select the gold bar, select **OK**, and a number of new expressions will be created.

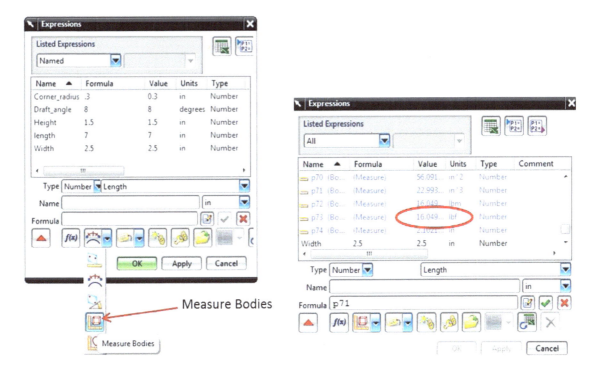

As you can see the weight of such a bar is 16.05 lbs. Not bad. Notice also that this activity creates a **Body Measurement** feature in the Part Navigator.

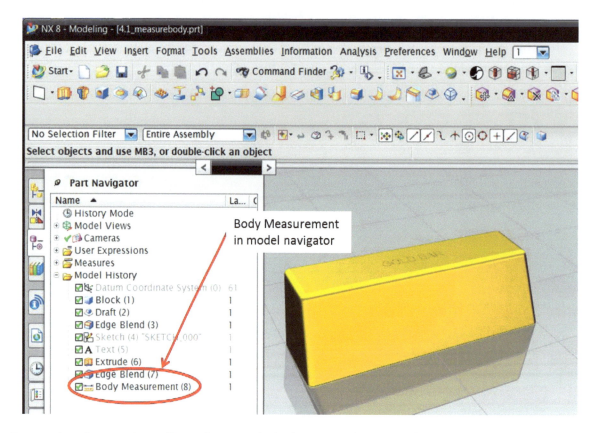

Next make a button that tells you how much the bar is worth. First make an expression that assumes the price of gold to be $1752 per ounce. We have about $28,000 per pound. Change the dimension to "**Constant**" and create a new expression "price=(whatever parameter is associated with the weight)*28,000". In this case it's P73 (lbf). Do not use lbm.

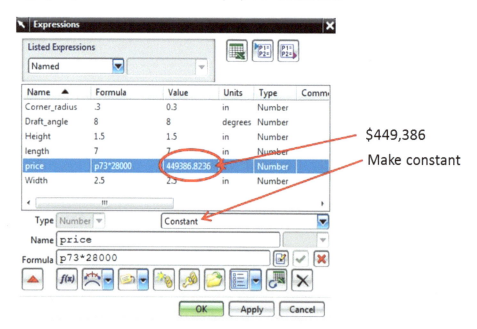

Finally, calculate what a 12 in length, by 4 inch wide by 4 inch high bar would be worth.

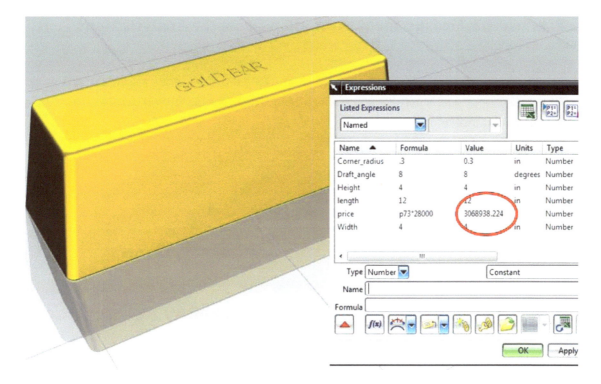

A mere 3 million dollars – not bad for a days work.

End of Exercise

Exercise 4.2: Measurement Expressions from the Analysis Menu

In this exercise you will learn how to create measurement expressions by using the **Analysis** menu. To proceed, open a new part file and create a sketch with a random shape made with a studio spline with a "**closed profile**".

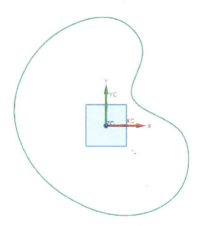

Next choose **Insert / Surface / Bounded plane**. Select the profile then **OK** and you will create a plane.

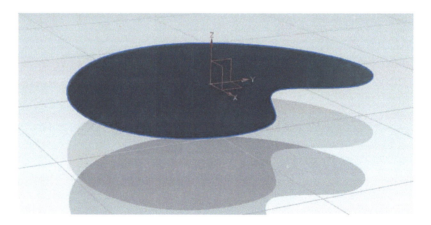

Next select **Analysis / Measure Face**, set the associativity switch to on and select the face.

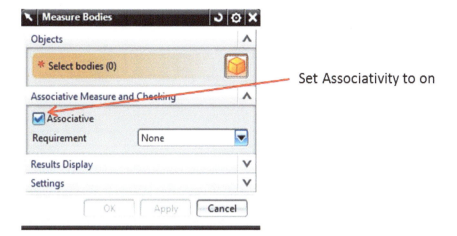

Set Associativity to on

Finally, select **Tools / Expression** or **Ctrl-E** and with the filter set to "**All**" you will see that there are now two new expressions:

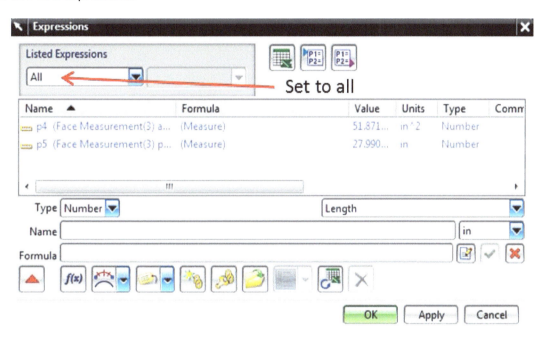

Set to all

End of Exercise

5. Expression Types

This section covers expression types. Expressions can be set to hold different value types such as a **string, number, boolean, integer, point, vector** or **list**.

String expressions are useful for holding a textual value. For instance if you have a jug you can use a string variable to imprint the word Gallons on the side as well as how many gallons it holds. To do this a user would create a model of a jug and create an expression called **raw_volume** that determines the volume. Next a variable called **gals** could be created.

The geometric expression **raw_volume** would be in units of inches cubed and converted into gallons. To do this a "**constant**" expression called **galamnt** could be set equal to **raw_volume**/231. Next a string expression called "**galtext**" would be created that holds the text "**Gallons**" plus the value of "**galamnt**". To get a textual value (a value that will appear as text) of **galamnt,** the operator "**ug_askExpressionValueAsString()**" can be used. In order to get the number to be an integer another function is used called **ceil()**. It rounds any number up to the next integer.

Thus the string variable will be set to a value of "**Gallons: 2**".

The final step is to imprint it onto the Jug. For this the **Text** command is used. Within the text command there is a check box called "**reference text**". With this button checked the text creation tool is ready to accept string variable expressions.

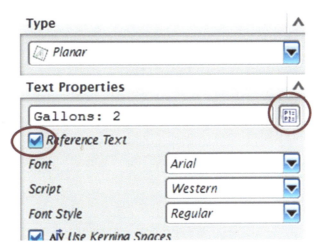

Next you need to choose the expression in the expressions list.

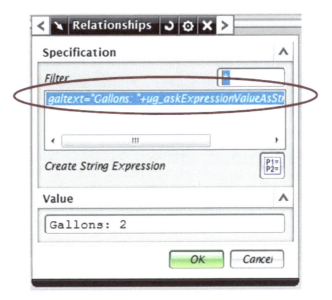

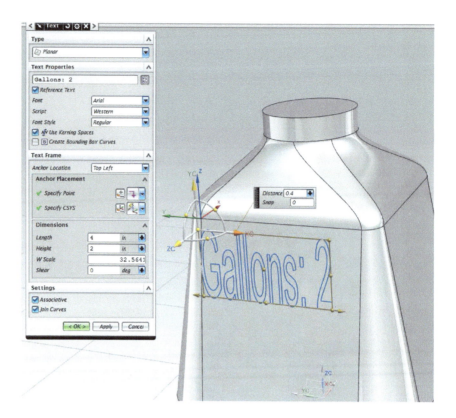

Now that you have the text curve with the gallons value you project the sketch onto the face of the model by going to **Insert -> Curves from Curves -> Project**. Select the text curve and the face of the model and hit **OK**.

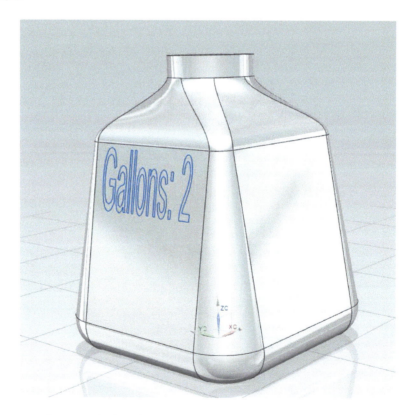

Next the lettering can be extruded and united.

Now if you go back into the model history and increase the size of this jug by 3 inches, NX will recalculate the measurements, update the expressions accordingly, and display the correct amount of gallons without ever having to go back and edit the text.

Now the model correctly displays 3 gallons since the height has been increased.

End of Exercise

Exercise 5.1: Using String Variables

Using what you've learned in the previous section you may now use a **String** expression to display a value that will change with the shape of the model as well as modify an expression to change the overall shape of the model.

First create a constant expression named **msize** with a value of 1. Then create the sketch below:

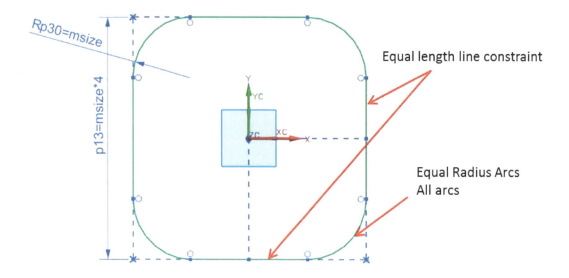

Finish the sketch and extrude using the expression **msize**. You can do this by selecting the dropdown icon next to the distance value, select formula and choose the **msize** expression. Next create a string expression named "**newtext**". The expression should be set in the manner shown in the diagram below:

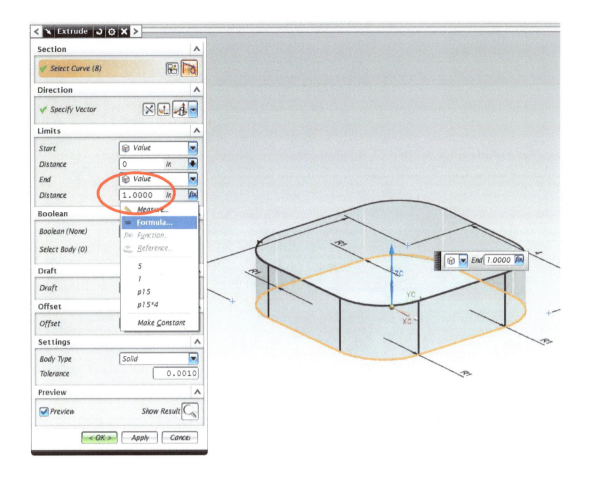

Now that you have an extruded sketch place the size variable onto the model. Using the steps covered in the previous section, create a text curve on the model that displays the following text "**Size: 1**"

Now that you have a block with the size value displayed on it, change the **msize** expression to equal 3 and select **Apply**.

End of exercise.

Exercise 5.2 Using Point Variables

NX has a really cool ability to capture the X, Y, and Z locations of points with one expression. Imagine being able to enter in a variable name such as "**point_1**"and entering the values 3, 5, and 0. Then, when you want to create a point at that location, you simply enter point_1 and the point is created. For example, try the following: In a new part file bring up the expression editor and set the expressions type to "**point**" as shown below.

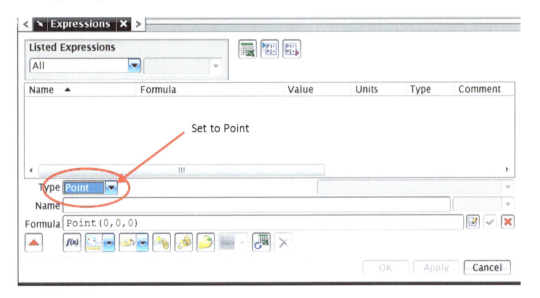

Next type in the name "**Cool_point**" or some other suitable name into the Name box. And type in 3,5, and 0 in the Formula box. It will appear as follows:

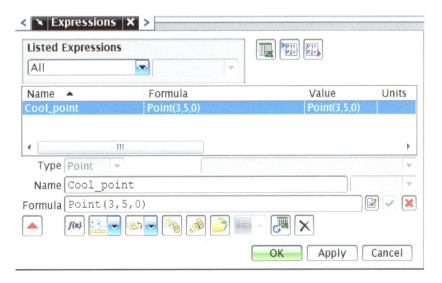

Once you select **Apply**, you've captured the location of the point. Now you may use it in a variety of places. You may use it as the start point of a cube or cylinder, a datum point location or the point to point move function in the synchronous modeling option. To practice the technique, create a small cylinder. Enter **Insert / Design Feature / Cylinder**. This will take you to the menu shown below where you can click on the point creation sub menu and choose the point you have created to be the start point of the cylinder.

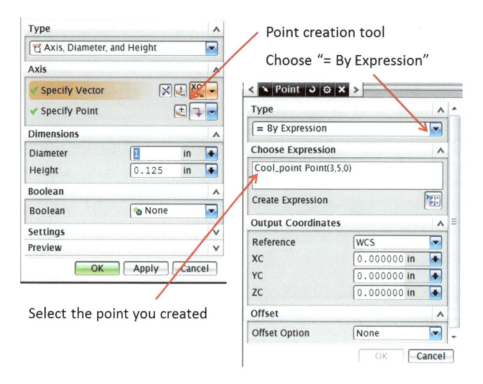

If you enter a diameter of **1** and a height of **1**, you will get a cylinder at the location shown below:

If you go to the expression editor and edit the location parameters of the point the cylinder will move. For example, change the parameters of the point you created to **-1, -2,** and **0**.

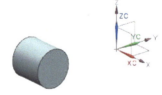

End of Exercise

Exercise 5.3 Using Vector Variables

Using an interaction similar to the last exercise you can create a vector expression. Imagine you were going to create a pipe who's start location was (0,0,0) and length was 10 feet long, diameter 8 inches in and had to be installed with a slope of one foot drop for every horizontal eight feet. To work the exercise, start a new inch part and bring up the expressions editor. Set the **Type** to **Vector** and input a variable name of **pipe_slope** and a formula value of **(8,-1,0)**.

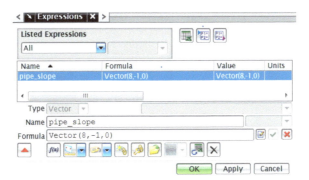

Next choose **Insert / Design Feature / Cylinder**

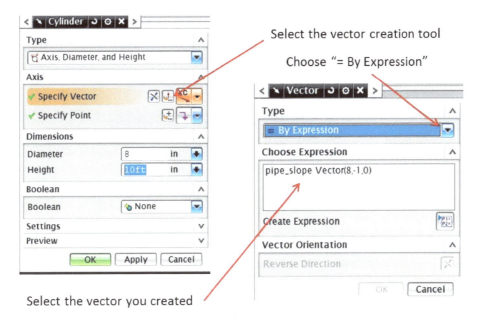

Select the vector creation tool

Choose "= By Expression"

Select the vector you created

Next enter the start point of (0,0,0) and select **Enter**.

End of exercise

Exercise 5.4 Adding Vectors and Points

Using the point type expression along with the vector type expression you can perform vector math calculations. Imagine you had a particle that started at a point location of (5,5,5) and a vector was applied to it that was described by (0,0,-5). The result would be a point located at (5,5,0). To work the exercise, start a part file and input the point "a=point(5,5,5)":

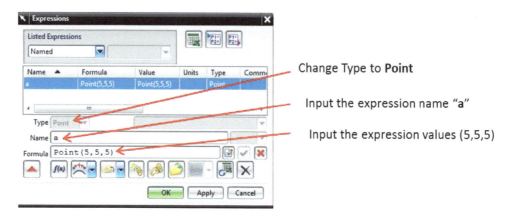

Change Type to **Point**

Input the expression name "**a**"

Input the expression values (5,5,5)

Next, input a vector and name it "**b**". Set the value to (0,0,-5)

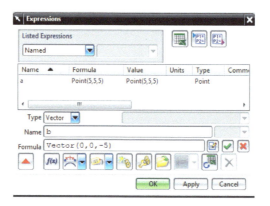

Finally create a point called c that equals a+b. The result should be (5,5,0)

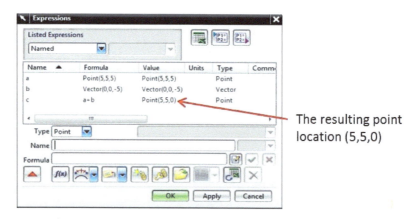

The resulting point location (5,5,0)

End of Exercise

Exercise 5.5 Adding Vectors

Imagine you need to know what the effective force is on a blade of a turbine blisk. You know that the lift force is 400 lbf, the drag force is 80 lbf and the centrifugal force is 500 lbf. What is the effective force? If we assume that the X axis represents the engine center line, the Y axis represents the vertical axis, and the Z the horizontal we can make the three vectors, add them and find out what the effective force is.

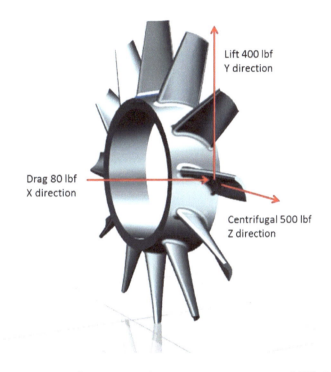

To proceed, open up a new part and execute ctrl-E. Input a vector named "**X**". Set it equal to **(80,0,0)**. Make a new vector and call it "**Y**". Set it equal to **(0,400,0)**. Next make one called "**Z**" and set it equal to **(0,0,500)**. Finally create a point called "**Result**" and set it equal to "**Point(0,0,0)+X+Y+Z**".

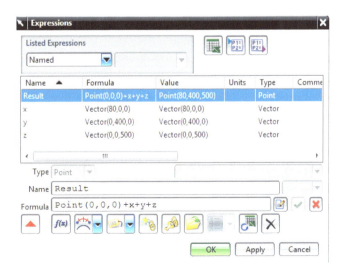

Next create a point using "**Result**". **Select** Insert **/ Datum /Point/ Point**.

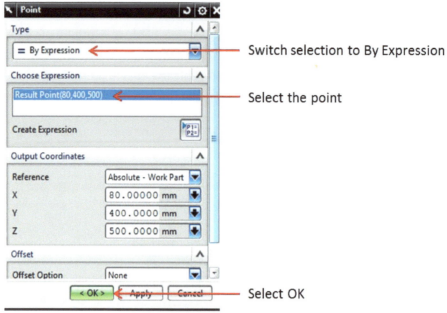

A point will be created. Finally, make a measurement expression for the point. Select **Analysis / Measure Distance/ Distance**. Select the origin point of the Datum CSYS and the new result point. The length is "**645 lbf**".

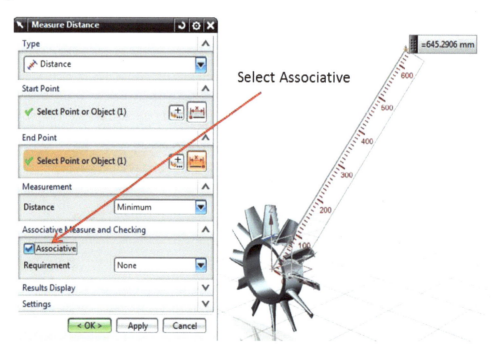

End of Exercise

6. Expressions Logic

This section covers how to use logic in the expression formula. Logic gives you the ability to have the model change in a nonlinear way based upon the state of other expressions. The key to creating logical statements is understanding the syntax. In a general sense the procedure is creating an expression that reads **X=if(some condition)then(Y)else(Z)**. At first glance this may be confusing but when broken down it has the following meaning. X is the variable that you are controlling. The condition is usually a comparison of two or more variables such as **A > B**, or **C<=D**. If the condition is true, then **X** is set to the value of **Y**, if not then **X** is set to the value of **Z**.

This ability it particularly useful when you are creating geometry whose dimensions change radically and based on those changes significant configuration changes are required. For example, consider a model of a dining table shown below:

An expression was created controlling the table length called **tablelen**. The desired logic has to do with the strength. When the table length exceeds a certain amount, in this case 8 feet, there must be another set of legs to support the middle. This is accomplished with a statement that controls the number of legs.

Number_of_legs=if(tablelen>=8ft)then(6)else(4)

Exercise 6.1 Using Incredibly Powerful Operators

The expressions logic language is augmented by some really neat programing operators. Here they are:

        <   means less than

        <=   means less than or equal to

        =   means equal to

        !=   means not equal to

        >   means greater than

        &   means <u>and</u>. For example if I wanted **X** to be equal to **5** if **A** equals **3** <u>and</u> **B** equals **5**.

        | means <u>or</u>. This one is tricky. It's the vertical bar that you get by pressing shift back slash

        -        means not

To use some of these operators in a realistic geometric example, imagine you are creating an assembly of a hatch way door. The hatch way will be used in many different locations on a rocket. There is a latch assembly that will be used on the opposite side of the hinges. When the door goes over 4 feet high, it needs more than one latch assembly. It also needs another latch assembly, if the operating pressure is higher than or equal to 50 psi. So the assembly that you create has an if-statement. The if-statement value is set to 1 (on) if height > 4ft or pressure is greater than or equal to 50, or the value is zero (off) if both the door height is less than 4ft and pressure less than 50.

To perform an example, create a new component called "**logic door**" and make the rectangular door shown below. It's important in this exercise that you get the name exactly right "**logic door**":

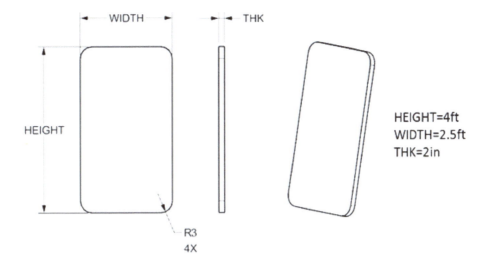

Next, make a new component called **latch**.

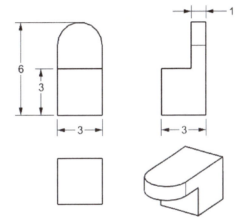

Create an assembly that has two latches assembled as shown below. The "**Distance**" assembly constraint should be used in order to place the latches 4 inches away from the edges.

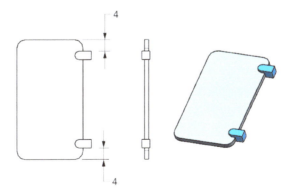

Next, navigate back into the door file and create the logic that you will need to indicate one or two latches.

Select **Tools / Expression**

and enter **pressure=40** (make sure it is a constant). Then enter
"**latch_switch=if(height>=4ft|pressure>=50)(1)else(0)**" (The vertical bar between **4ft** and **pressure** is a shift back slash). The value given to **latch_switch** will become **0** since the pressure is only **40** and the height is only **3.5ft**.

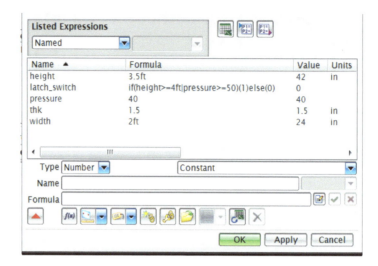

Next, the **latch_switch** has to be used inside the assembly file to turn off one of the instances of the latch and move the one that remains to the center. Make the assembly the work part and enter into the expressions editor **a="logic door"::latch_switch.** The words "**logic door**" in quotes indicates to NX that you will be getting the value from the part file logic door, and the :: indicates that you will be receiving the value of latch_switch. This is called an interpart expression. It will be covered more fully in a later chapter.

Next, enter in to the expressions editor **h="logic door"::height**. This will enable you to use the height of the door to move the bottom component to the middle when there is just one latch. The expressions editor should now appear as shown below:

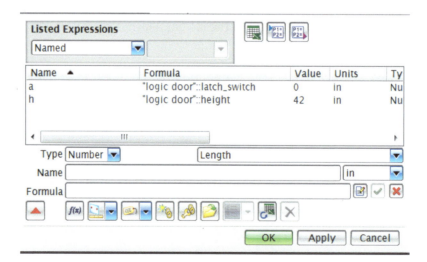

Next, activate the assembly navigation tool, select the top latch component as shown below, right click to bring up the menu and select "**suppression**".

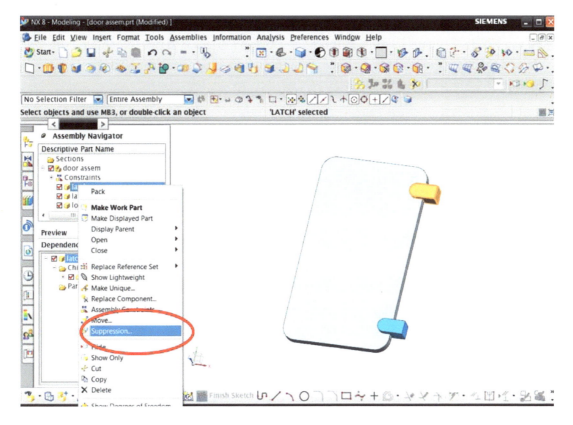

Within the **Suppression** menu, click on "**Controlled by Expression**" and enter "**a**".

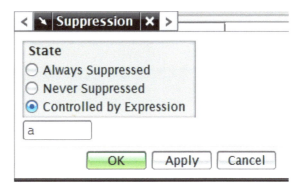

Since the value of **a** is 0 (off) the top latch component will disappear upon selecting **OK.** The assembly will appear as shown below:

Finally, you need one more expression. The distance constraint for the bottom latch needs to be set to a value of (**h/2**) minus half the width of the latch to move it into the center. Find the expression that was made for the lower latch distance in this case it is **p0**. Replace the value of 4 with **if(a=0)(h/2-1.5)else(4)**

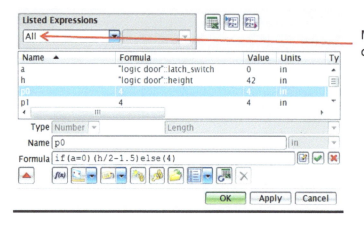

Make sure this says **All** so you can see all the dimensions

The result will be an assembly with one latch in the middle of the door.

Now test the logic. If the pressure goes to **60** and height goes to **2ft** what happens?

What happens when **height** is **6ft** and pressure is **10**?

End of exercise

Exercise 6.2: Using Logic Expressions -2

In this exercise we will have NX choose between two standard cross sections of beams based on the weight of a load that will be welded to it in cantilever, and the length of the beam. Imagine that the 2 beams that you have in stock are size 1 (2 inches wide and 3 inches tall), or size 2 (3 inches wide and 8 inches tall).

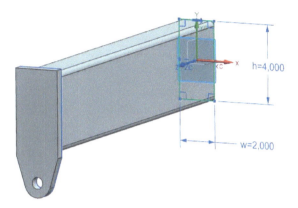

To begin the exercise, create a sketch that has a width and a height variable set to 2 and 4 respectively. Extrude the sketch with an expression that says **l=18**. Place .2 radius blends on all the edges as shown and shell the beam by **.125**. It's not entirely necessary but you may want to place the little structure on the end as shown in the diagram above.

Next you may create an expression for the weight on the beam. In the expressions editor create an expression "**weight=500**". Make it a constant. Also make an expression for the moment on the beam, the expression should read **Moment=l*weight**. Make this one a constant too. The **l** is the length expression that you created when you extruded the bar. Your expression editor should resemble the sample below:

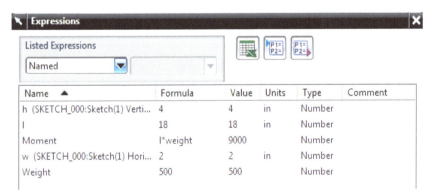

Assume that when the moment is over **20,000** the assembly must change to the larger cross section.

Next create an expression that reads "**w=if(moment>20000)then(3)else(2)**" and another expression that reads "**h=if(moment>20000)then(8)else(3)**".

With a weight of **500** lbs. the model selects size 1 as shown below.

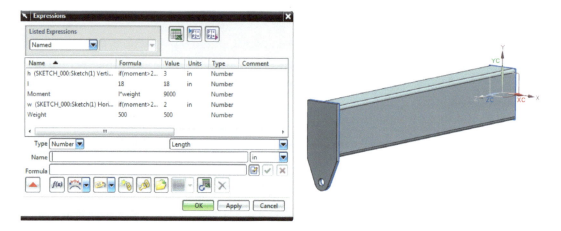

With a weight of **1200** lbs. the model selects the larger cross section (size 2) as shown below.

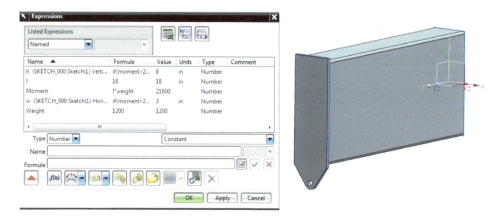

With a weight of **700** lbs. and a length of **40** inches size 2 is selected again as shown below.

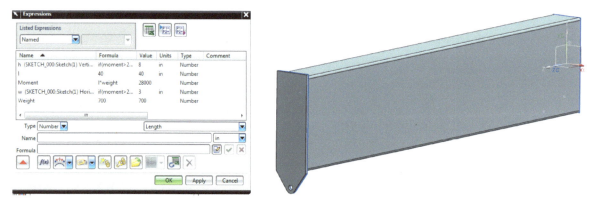

End of Exercise

Exercise 6.3: Using Logic Expressions -3

For this exercise you will use a lot of what you've learned in previous sections by creating a logical expression that uses the string expression.

First create an expression for length as shown below.

Next create the sketch shown below:

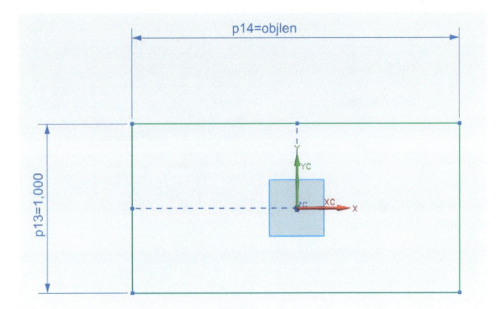

Use the expression **objlen** for the length of this sketch. Now finish the sketch and extrude it by 0.2in.

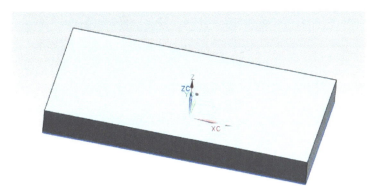

Now that you have a block that is controlled lengthwise by the **objlen** expression you may create a string expression using logical expressions.

Open the expression editor and create a string expression called **objdisplay**.

Using what you've learned from the previous sections, create a logical formula that displays "**cm: 2.54*objlen**" if **objlen** falls below 1, then have it display "**in: objlen**" if **objlen** is under 12 and then finally have it display "**ft: objlen/12**" if **objlen** is greater than or equals 12.

Next add a text curve to the face of your model, use the **objlen** expression to set the width of the text, and then use the **objdisplay** expression as the actual text itself as shown below:

Having created your logical string expression if you change the **objlen** expression to go below 1 it should produce the following:

Likewise if we change the value of **objlen** to be above 12 it will produce the following:

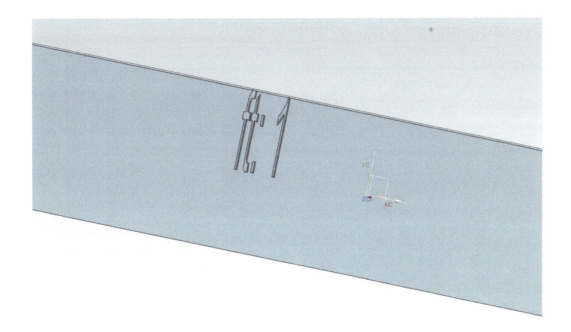

Now you may have a cool string expression that can change its displayed unit of measurement based upon the length of the model.

Hint!

This logical expression is fairly difficult to build, so to help out here is the expression we used.

if(objlen<1)("cm: "+ug_askExpressionValueAsString(2.54*objlen, ""))else if(objlen>=12)("ft: "+ug_askExpressionValueAsString(objlen/12, "")) else ("in: "+ug_askExpressionValueAsString(objlen, ""))

Also for aligning the text to the face of the model without causing problems at certain small sizes I used this logical expression to control the text height.

if(objlen<1)(.5*objlen)else(p32/2)

The expression **p32** was the width along the YC vector.

End of Exercise

7. Feature Suppression by Expression

There are geometric situations that dictate a higher degree of parametric ability than simple expressions can handle. For example, in the model of a water tank shown below, based on the internal volume and therefor the overall weight, a different type of crane loop is used. In the figure below a 3ft diameter by four foot long tank has an internal volume of approximately 172 gallons. The weight of the water is about 1441 lbs. and the weight of the vessel with hatch covers is 679 lbs. for a total of 2120 lbs. With the total weight less than 3000 lbs., simple loops welded onto the vessel component will suffice.

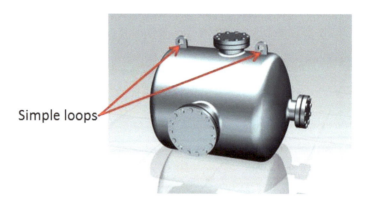

Simple loops

When the tank is 8ft long the water weight jumps up to 3109 lbs. and the weight of the vessel is 1061 for a total of 4170 lbs. The loops are no longer adequate and are replaced with bands and blocks as shown below.

In order to bring this astonishing amount of design logic to your modeling you need to create three unique expression entities; You need to create a "**measurement expression**" that calculates the weight of the water and tank combined, an if-statement to test to see if the overall weight is over the threshold of 3000 lbs., and a switch expression that will be used to control **feature suppression by expression** entities.

To create a geometric expression you select **Tools / Expression** / to bring up the Expression dialog, then you select the "**Measure Bodies**" icon and click on the body that you want a geometric expression for.

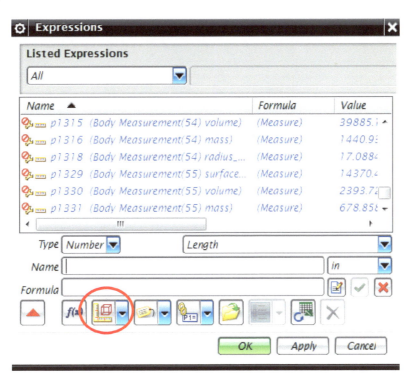

Once you've selected the body, parameters for the **volume, mass, radius of gyration, weight, volume, and surface area** will appear in the expressions editor. You may re-name the various quantities to make them a bit easier to spot. Note: you must have a separate body that models the water inside.

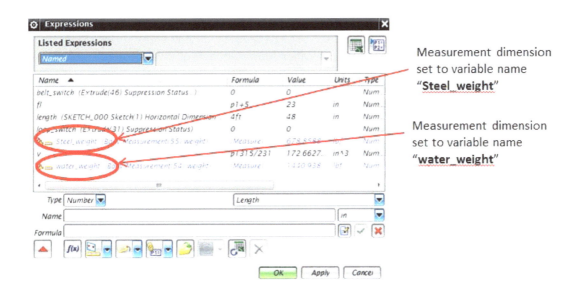

Measurement dimension set to variable name "**Steel_weight**"

Measurement dimension set to variable name "**water_weight**"

To proceed, the model must be made with the simple loops and an expression must be made that controls their suppression state. In this case a variable called "**loop_switch**" was created. The procedure is easy; you select **Edit / Feature / Suppress by Expression**. The following menu appears:

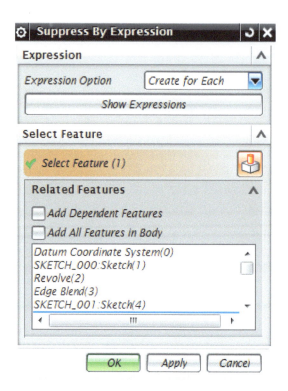

When you select the feature that corresponds to the tabs, you are able to add any dependent features if necessary. This could be blends or holes etc. When you select **Apply**, you may then find the identity of the expression that is created by selecting the **"Show Expressions"** button. The new expression is then set equal to the variable called loop switch, thus giving you full control over the tabs with the simple expression that you had created.

Once done with creating loop switch and the feature suppression variable, you would manually set it equal to zero so the loops would suppress leaving room for you to create models of the blocks and straps. You repeat the process of making the feature suppression variable for the straps and then you have the two switches. "**loop_switch**" and "**strap_switch**".

To finish off the model, you simply create a logical expression that varies the switches as a function of the measurement variables "**Water_weight**" and "**Steel_weight**" and you are done. Assuming the overall weight threshold to be 3000 lbs., the two expressions are:

Loop_switch=if(Steel_weight+water_weight>3000)then(0)else(1)

Belt_switch=if(Steel_weight+water_weight>3000)then(1)else(0)

Exercise 7.1 Feature Suppression by Expression

In this example you will practice using the **feature suppression by expression** technique in conjunction with the logic capability. The gist of this example is one of a large plate that is to have a loop welded on to it right in the middle. When the plate's weight exceeds a limit of 6,000 lbs., there must be two loops welded to the plate instead of just one, and they have to be positioned on the ends instead of in the middle.

To proceed, create a large plate using the block command. Use **Insert / Design Feature / Block**. Make it **5ft** wide, **10ft** tall, and **2in** thick. The default density of material in NX is **.2829 lbs./in³**, roughly the density of cold rolled steel. The weight is therefore $(10 \times 12) \times (5 \times 12) \times 2 \times .2829 = 4073.76$ lbs.

Next create a geometric expression for the weight. **Tools / Expressions / Measure Bodies**. In this case **p19** is the resulting force at **4073.76**.

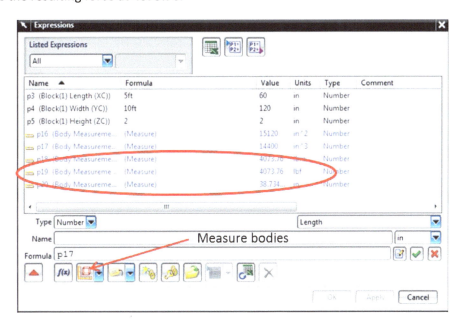

Next, create a sketch on the face of the plate and at the top edge as shown below:

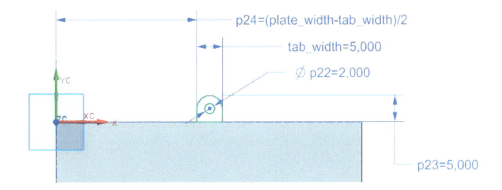

As you create the dimensions for the sketch, make sure the width of the tab is called **tab_width** and set it equal to **5**. Also make sure the width of the plate (5 feet) is set to a nice expression such as **plate_width**. Now position the tab right in the center by creating the dimension shown in the previous diagram as **p24** and entering in **(plate_width-tab_width)/2**.

Next, extrude the tab rearward to match the 2 inch plate thickness, and unite.

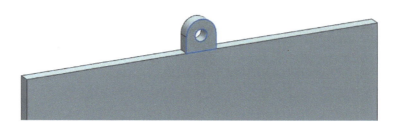

Next, create a switch for the tab to be centered or at the end, based on the weight. Use **Tools / Expressions** and enter **B=if(p19<=6000)then((plate_width-tab_width)/2)else(0)**. (You will need to make it a constant. Now set p24 equal to B (**p24=B**)

Next, create a switch that you will use later to turn on and off the second loop if **weight** exceeds **6000**. If the value of the switch is **1**, the second loop will be on, and it will be off if the value goes to zero. Enter the expression **switch=if(p19>6000)then(1)else(0)**

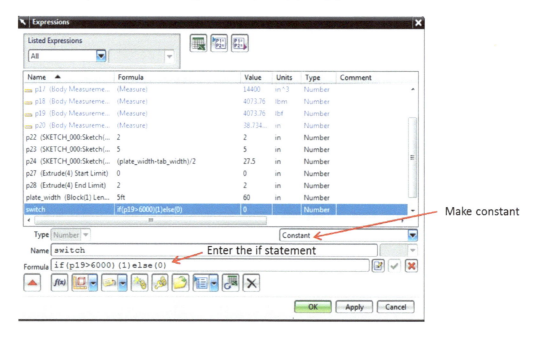

Next, change the length of the plate from 10ft to 15ft. The weight will become 6110.64 lbs. and **B** will equal **0**. The tab will move all the way to the side.

Next make a center datum plane and mirror the feature over to the other side.

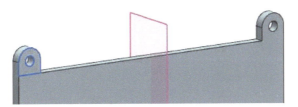

Next, create a **feature suppression by expression** entity for the mirror feature. **Use Edit Feature / Suppress by Expression.**

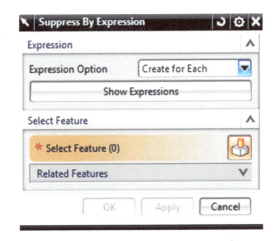

Select the mirror feature and click on **Apply**. Once done, click on the **Show Expression** button to find out the name of the new feature suppression by expression.

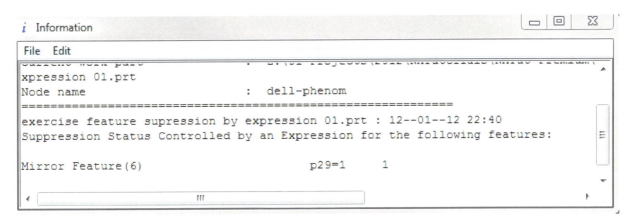

In this case **P29** is the new expression.

Finally you may link **P29** to the "**switch**" expression that you created previously. Once done you should test your model. Let the height be 4ft: (1629) lbs.

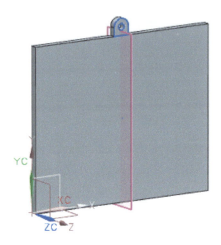

What happens when the width is 15ft and the height is 8ft?

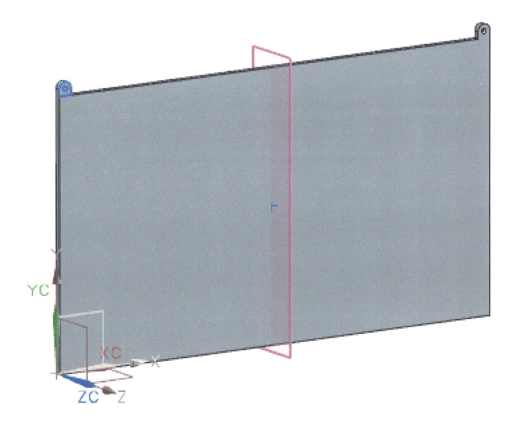

Success!

End of exercise

8. Using Math Functions

The math functions that are available in NX cover almost everything that you may want to calculate while making a CAD model. This includes all the trigonometric functions such as sin, cosine, tangent and the like, plus all other arithmetic functions such as the natural log, absolute value, etc. In short everything that is included on a scientific calculator and more. In most cases you use them by typing in the name of the function then left parenthesis, the argument, then right parentheses. For example **sin(45)** will return a value of **.7071**, **tan(45)** will return a value of **1**. You may even create your own custom functions.

You can use math functions in the expressions editor or you can type them in when you are creating features. For example, there is a function called "**round**". It does exactly what you would expect. For any argument that it is given, it returns the nearest integer value. In the following example two values of a sketch are used to specify the rounded value of an extrusion length of a solid, **p0=2.3**, the shorter side of the sketch bellow and **p1=3.65** the longer side. The extrusion distance is typed in as **round(p0+p1)**. As you can see the result is exactly **6** rather than 5.95.

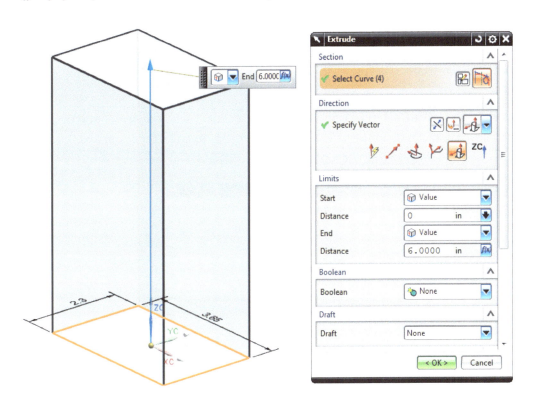

If you are having trouble remembering what a particular math function is called, or are looking for one that you've never used, you can click on the function button in the expressions editor $f(x)$. Once there, you can choose the "**math**" category by clicking on the down arrow to the right of the category menu. The resulting display will show you all the math functions that are available. There are about 22 in all.

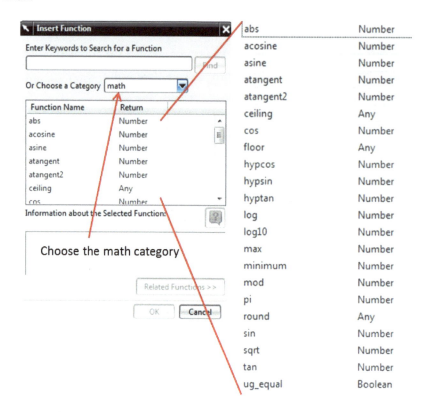

When you select one of the functions, you will also receive a detailed explanation of the function and it's use if available. Clicking on the button that reads "**Related functions**" will show you just that.

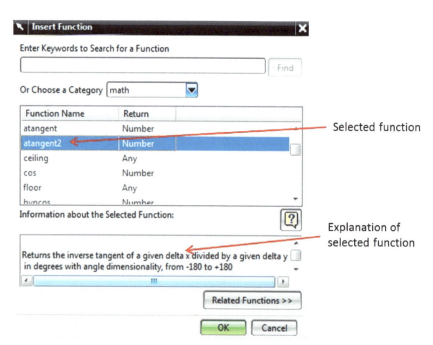

Exercise 8.1 Using Math Functions

In this exercise a straight length of molding is created that is to be fit around a disc. The diameter of the disc starts at 5 inches and may be subject to change; therefore the length of the molding is equal to the circumference. The circumference is obtained by multiplying the diameter by that loveliest of lovely constants, pi. In order to proceed create a cylinder with a 5 inch diameter, and a half inch height. It will appear as shown below:

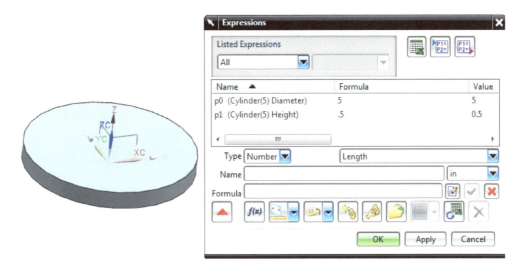

IF you started with a new part file, the diameter of your cylinder will probably be represented by **p0**. The next task is to create an expression that will represent the length of the molding. Instead of typing in the number 3.14 for pi you can use the mathematical function in NX to get a highly accurate value. From the **Tools / Expression** menu select the **Function** button. Choose the "**math**" choice in the **Categories** pull down and scroll down to where **pi** appears.

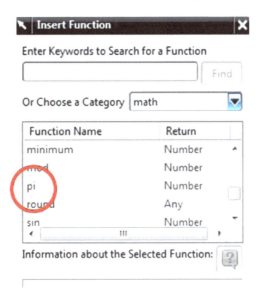

When you click on **pi** in the scroll down menu, the function for pi "**pi()**" will load itself into the expression creation tool as shown below:

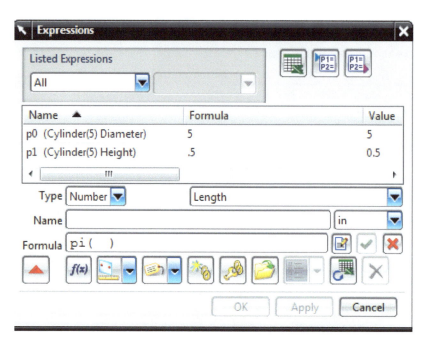

Add in the expression name and the multiplication of p0.

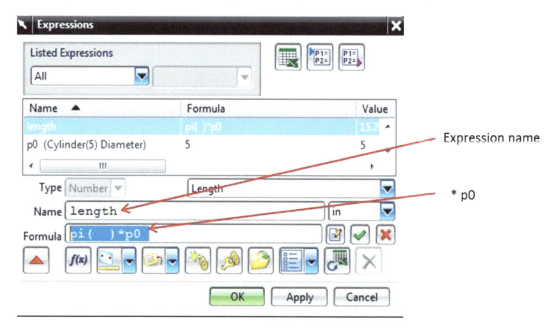

Once you have made a variable called **length**, you may create a profile of the molding and revolve it around the cylinder. Then you may extrude the same profile using the length variable as the end distance of an extrude to see what the molding looks like when it's all straightened out.

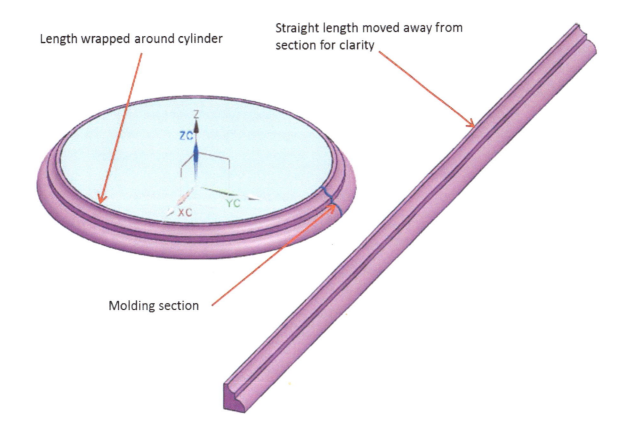

Length wrapped around cylinder

Straight length moved away from section for clarity

Molding section

End of exercise

Exercise 8.2 Create Your Own Custom Function

This section teaches you how to create your own custom function. Although the number of formulas available in NX is pretty high, there are still occasions when you might want to create your own function. For example imagine you had a need to create a function for Mach number, Reynolds number, Prandtl number or perhaps finding the pressure of a gas at a given volume and temperature. You first create a file with the extension ".dfa". You code it to capture the mathematical relationship you desire, then you save it in the appropriate directory. Once there, and a few simple procedures it is available for you to use right within NX. For this to work, you must have a Knowledge Fusion license.

To proceed with the exercise we must have a simple equation to emulate. Here's one from that seminal text on machine design by M.F. Spotts – *Design of Machine Elements*. Page 138 equation (8) states that Horse power = Torque in inch lbs. times rotations per minute divided by 63,025. If we multiply that by .7457 we get kilowatts. So the simple equation becomes. KW=.7457*(rpm*torque/63025). Where torque is in in-lbs.

The first step is to open up a note pad or similar editor and create a file with the name of your function with a ".dfa" file type. It is important to name the file well because the text before the .dfa will determine what will appear in the "Category" section of the expression editor.

You may call your example shaft_power.dfa.

Next, you must make sure that the first line in your file has the following text:

#! UGNX/KF 3.0

These characters let NX know that **Knowledge Fusion** will be used. Knowledge fusion is the code that allows NX to react in mathematically sophisticated ways.

The Next line that should appear will define the function name. In this case the function name will be shaft_power.

Defun: shaft_power (

The next 2 lines will signal to NX that the new function will be visible to "DesignLogic" (the expressions capability in NX).

#+
DesignLogic=yes

The next line is the description. It will actually show up in the box titled **Information about the Selected Function** in the expression menu. The format is whatever appears in between the two sets of characters #. and .#. The lines of code look like the following:

Description:

#.
The inputs are T the torque measured in inch-lbs and n, the revolutions per minute
This function will return the output answer in kilowatts
.#

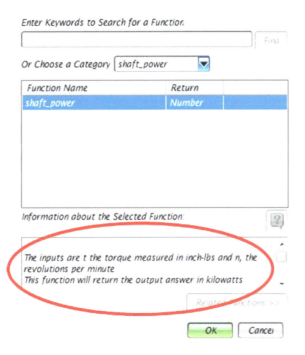

The next lines identify the mathematical inputs with comments at the end of each line. Then calculates the result and returns it to NX. Whatever you place inside the brackets will be calculated. The format is

@{ what ever is calculated }

The lines of code are as follows:

```
#-
number $t;    # constant -  #. T measured in inch lbs. .#
number $n;    # constant -  #. n measured in revs per minute .#
)
@{
       $value  << ($t*$n/63025);
} number;
```

Additional comments are used to provide text that will be presented to the user as labels in the **Insert Function** dialog and the **Function Arguments** dialog. For example the program will contain the following:

#. Returns a number that represents the power in kilowatts.#

You can see this string above in the first image that is part of this exercise, near the bottom of the dialog. The strings "T measured in inches lbs." and "n measured in revs per minute" also appear in the **Function Arguments** dialog shown below.

Finish the function with the lines of code that define the related commands and the end of the program as shown below in the full text of a file that was made for this example.

The full text of the file is as follows:

```
shaft_power.dfa - Notepad

File  Edit  Format  View  Help
#! NX/KF 3.0

###########################################################################

Defun: shaft_power(
#+
DesignLogic=yes
------------------------------------------------------------------------
Description:
#.
The inputs are t the torque measured in inch-lbs and n, the revolutions per minute
This function will return the output answer in kilowatts
.#
------------------------------------------------------------------------
#-
number   $t;      # constant - #.T measured in inch lbs. .#
number   $n       # constant - #.n measuted in revolutions per minute.#
)
@{
    $value << (.7457*$t*$n/63025);
    } number;

#+
------------------------------------------------------------------------
Returns:
power - #.Returns a number that represents the power in kilowatts.#

See Also:
------------------------------------------------------------------------
#-

# EOF
```

Finally the file must be located in the appropriate place and made available to NX. There are two ways. The first way is best for testing and development. You simply access **Tools / Knowledge Fusion / DFA Manager** and add a "search" directory.

To proceed, click on "**Browse**" then navigate to the location of your file.

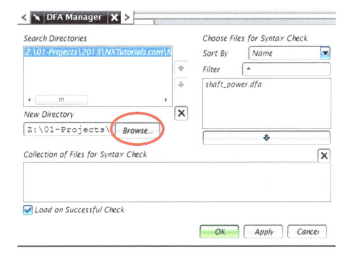

Next use the down arrow button to drop it from the list on the right into the box below labeled "**Collection of Files for Syntax Check**". Then check the "**Load on Successful Check**" box and "**Apply**".

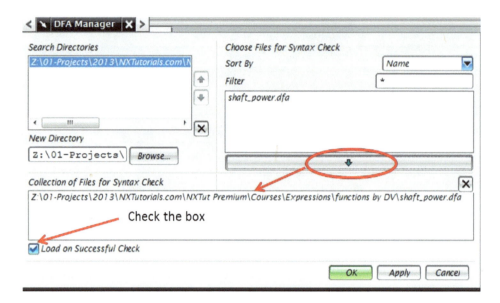

If there are no errors, you will receive a message stating, "**There are no errors found when checking DFA Syntax and loading files**".

The new function will now be available inside the expressions "**Insert Function**" dialog.

Now the real fun begins. Open up a new part file and select **Tools / Expression** Click on the functions button $f(x)$. Click on the down arrow to the right of the "**Choose a Category**" box and find the new **shaft_power** function. (For reference, the category names here are taken from the name of the DFA file containing the function or set of functions.)

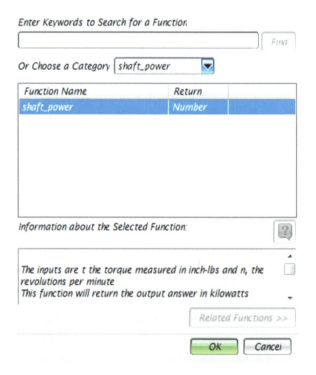

Upon selecting the new function you will get prompted for the inputs as shown below:

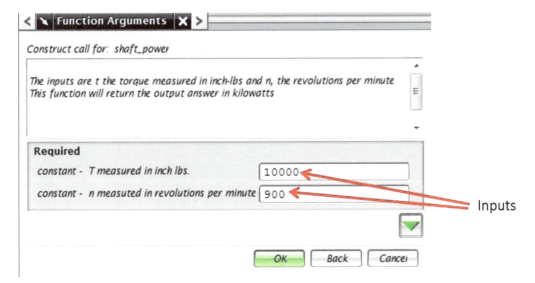

When you use the new function it is can be crucial to select the correct type Dimensions and units. In this example, you may select Power, and Kilowatts. Then you can enter a new expression name for the result and select **OK.**

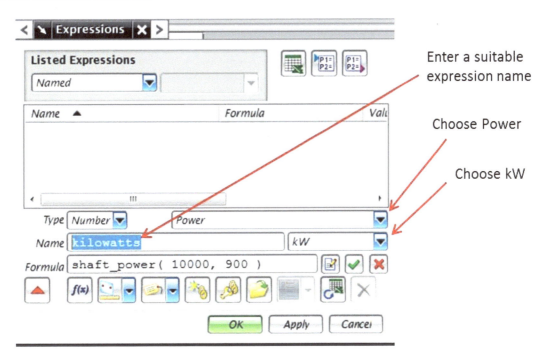

When you select OK, you will have the expression that gives you the answer.

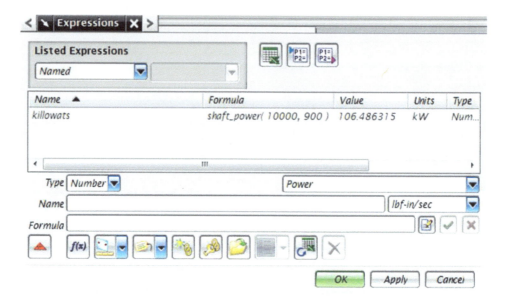

There is another way to deploy your functions for a broader audience. Here are the details:

Broader Deployment (This method essentially uses the classic approach for plugging customizations into NX.)

a)   Set up a folder within which you will package your customization for deployment (may contain special folders like "startup", "application", "udo", etc.)

b)   Create a folder called "dfa" inside this folder. (This is a special folder just like "application" and "startup", and Knowledge Fusion classes and functions contained within this folder will be added as KF system classes (as opposed to user classes) at NX startup time.

c)   Put your DFA file in the "dfa" folder.

d)   Aim one of the standard environment variables at your top-level customization folder [either in the OS or in a startup script]

      a.   UGII_USER_DIR

      b.   UGII_SITE_DIR

      c.   UGII_VENDOR_DIR

      d.   UGII_CUSTOM_DIRECTORY_FILE
      (pointed to a custom_dirs.dat file containing your directory)

e)   Start NX. :-)

f)   The new function should be available inside the Expressions "Insert Function" dialog at that point.

Once your function is tested and working (using option 1 above) and you want to deploy it more permanently using option 2, just remember to remove the search path from the DFA Manager dialog. Also, if you get a chance and what you've written is not proprietary, please try to upload it to NXTutorials.com and share it with the entire NX user community.

For reference, all of the DFA files defining the out-of-the-box functions are available in the NX install for you to inspect and plagiarize freely. If you decide to use an existing DFA file as the basis for your own new function(s), then be sure to copy the out-of-the-box file to a new location, rename it to something new, and use the methods above to tell NX where to find it. Editing the out-of-the-box functions directly is not a great idea, and adding your own new functions directly to the NX installation will actually *not* work. For performance reasons, NX already "knows about" all of the out-of-the-box functions in the default installation, and will not try to search the system directories for any new functions other than these.

End of Exercise

9. Amazing Shapes Using Expressions in Law Curves

The law curve is one of the coolest, most powerful yet weirdest abilities that is contained in NX. The idea is you create an expression "**t=1**" then you create an expression for the x direction (**XT=blah blah blah**), create an expression for the y direction (**YT=blah blah blah**) then create an expression for the z direction (**ZT = whatever**). Once you have all the expressions in place you access the law curve dialog and a curve is created that is as amazing as your imagination and math skills will allow. Buckminster Fuller would have had a field day. As an example, if you input the following expressions then create a tube entity on the result, it will take on the shape shown below:

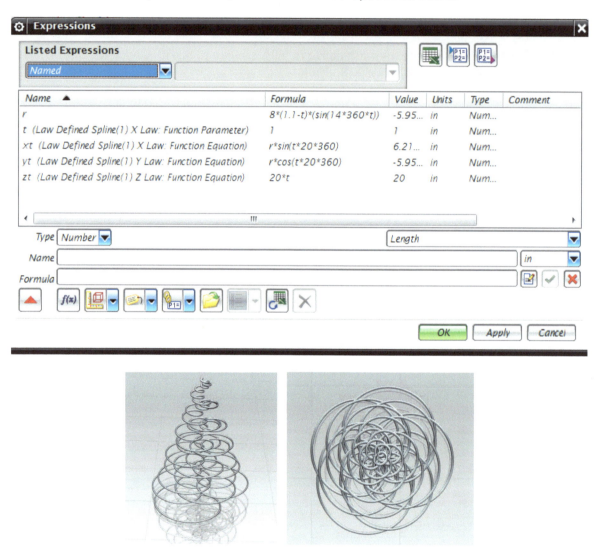

To understand it a bit better imagine that during the creation of a law curve the variable "**t**" will go through a million increments from 0 to 1. Each increment will be assigned to each of the expressions, **XT, YT and ZT** and a point will be created. When it finally gets to 1 and all the points are created all the points are joined with a spline. The inner workings of the law curve are a bit recondite but it is a great way to create curves that are like no other. They are accurate and bullet proof.

Exercise 9.1: Creating a Law Curve

In this exercise you will create an 18 inch diameter parabolic mirror with a focal point that is 20 inches away from the center. To begin you will need the correct parametric equations. The basic formula will be **Y=.0125 × X²**

Select Tools/ Expressions

Enter **t=1, xt=t*9, yt=.0125*xt^2, zt=0**

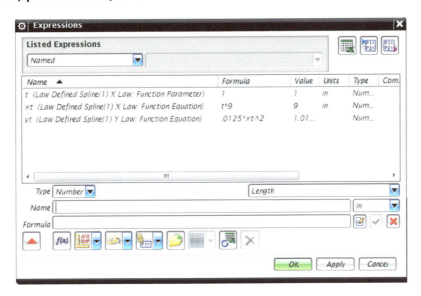

Select **Insert / Curve / Law Curve**

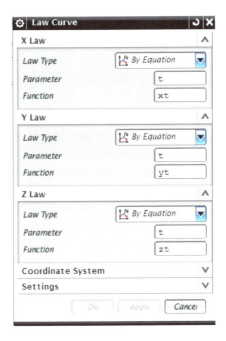

Upon selecting **Enter**, the curve will be created

In order to verify the focal distance, you can create a sketch on top of the curve as shown below. The sketch is drawn 90 degrees CCW for clarity. A single horizontal line is drawn that represents a photon of light striking the parabola. Then a line is drawn perpendicular to the parabola to represent the angle of incidence. A circle is drawn to control the line representing light reflecting off the parabola. The two lines are made tangent to the circle to ensure that the angle of reflection is equal to the angle of incidence. When the end of the line representing the reflection is constrained to being along the Y axis (using a point on curve constraint) it indicates the exact location of the focal point.

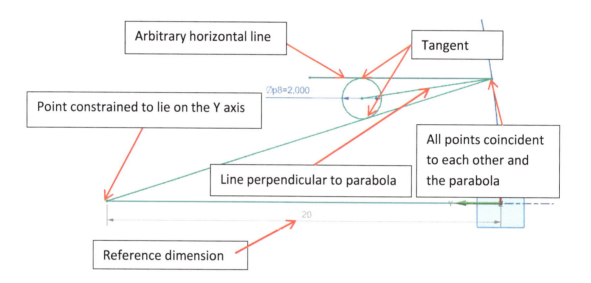

Once the sketch is created you can move the arbitrary line that represents a photon of light anywhere along the parabola and the focal point should remain the same.

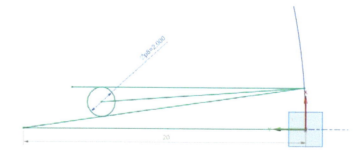

The next step is to create a revolved solid from the parabola. The revolve tool is used and the Body Type is set to **"Sheet"**.

The diagram shows a sphere placed at the focal point.

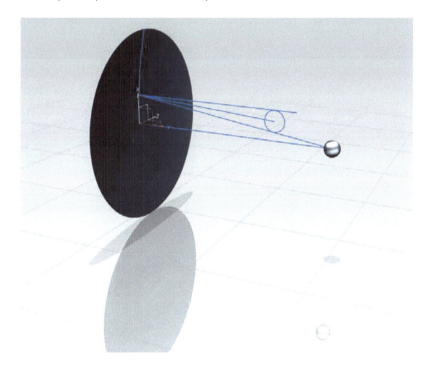

End of Exercise

Exercise 9.2: Creating a Law Curve for a Transducer Component

Some companies that design and manufacture speakers use the terminology transducer. Within a transducer there is a component called a spider. It's depicted on the diagram that was downloaded from the internet as component 5:

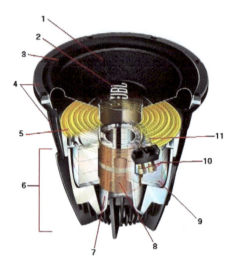

The spider can be depicted as a sinusoid that is revolved around an axis. To proceed, create the following equations in the expression editor:

- t=1
- h=.2*(1.15-t)
- xt= 1+t*3
- yt=h*sin(t*5*360)
- zt=0
- thk=.02

Once you have input all the expressions, and you have created a law curve, you may revolve it and thicken the result by "**thk**". The result will appear as shown below:

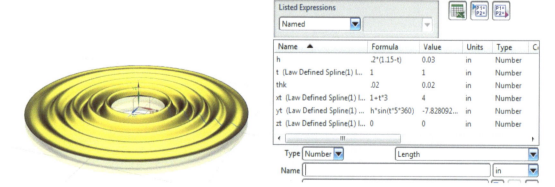

End of Exercise

10. Creating Interpart Expressions

When creating an assembly with parts that fit together, it is extremely powerful to link dimensions of one component to those of another. The dimensions are represented by expressions called **interpart expressions**. An interpart expression reference essentially "pulls" a value from an expression in another part into an expression in the work part, setting up a parent-child relationship between these two expressions – and so when the parent expression changes, the child will also update to reflect the same value. These interpart expressions can be created between "sibling" assembly components, or they can describe relationships between an assembly components and an upper level assembly.

Note: A situation that should be avoided is creating a "Circular Reference". A circular reference is caused when two expressions reference each other. For example Expression_A contains a formula that references Expression_B, while Expression_B's formula contains a reference to Expression_A, causing a recursive loop. NX will make attempts to recognize these occurrences to actively prevent you from introducing them into your assemblies.

Interpart expressions can be created manually or you can use the tool that is located at the bottom of the Expressions editor. A newer tool in the Expressions dialog in the very latest versions of NX can also help you create multiple interpart expressions at once – a somewhat common workflow in creating robust larger-scale parametric assemblies.

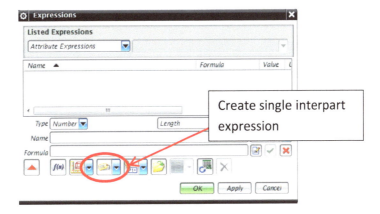

When two components are linked together with interpart expressions they automatically communicate when both components are open at the same time. When a part containing an interpart expression is open, and the part that it is linked to is not, the interpart expression simply remains set at the same value as when the two parts were last open together.

In the example assembly shown below two models are created that fit together. In the female component there is an expression called "Hole" that controls the diameter of the hole. In the male component there is a corresponding dimension called Pole. The value of the Pole dimension is set to "female"::Hole. The fact that female is in quotes indicates that female is the part file containing the expression being referenced. The "::" is the operator that indicates that what follows is an expression within the part file of the name "female"

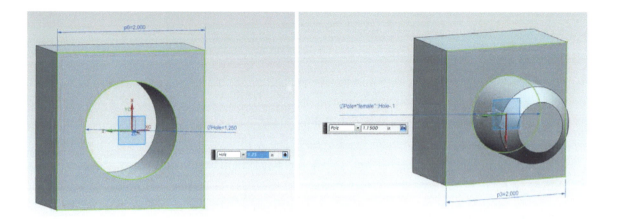

In the example above the assembly appears as shown below:

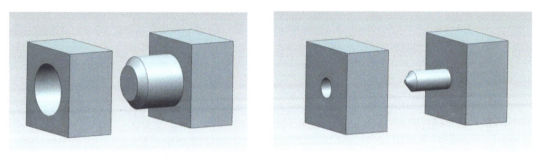

Hole = 1.25   Hole =.5

The following figure shows what an interpart expression looks like in the expressions editor.

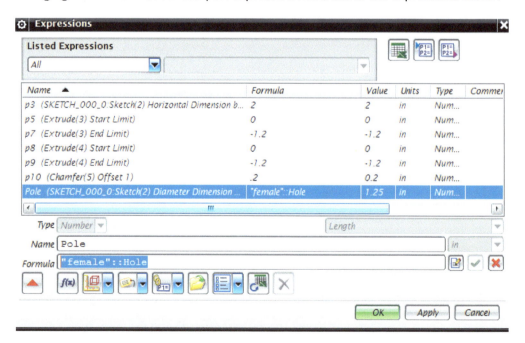

Exercise 10.1: Creating Interpart Expressions

In this exercise you will learn how to use the interpart expression editor and create a parametric link between two or more part files. The first step is to create a part file called **Glass**. In that part file create a block. As you input the values input **l=20** then enter, **w=12** then enter, **thk=.25** then enter. This will simultaneously create the expression l,w, and thk as it creates the block that conforms to it. This block represents the glass.

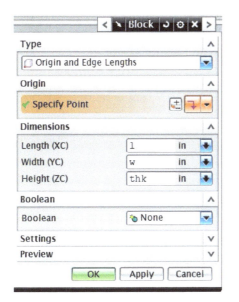
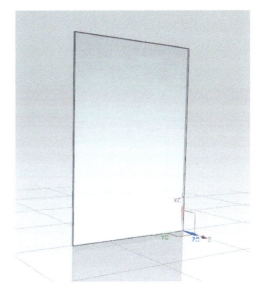

Next create a new component part file that will be called **Frame**. Soon the window frame will be perfectly matched to the glass using the interpart expressions. The first entity to create in the new part file is a sketch that is open-ended and dimensioned as shown below.

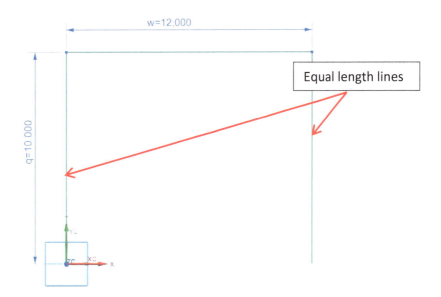

On the left hand end of the first sketch add a new sketch that is on an orthogonal plane.

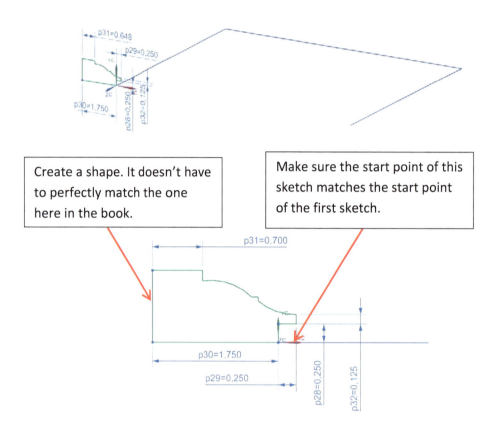

Create a shape. It doesn't have to perfectly match the one here in the book.

Make sure the start point of this sketch matches the start point of the first sketch.

Use the **Sweep Along A Guide** function to create a solid. This is a half of the frame. Use **Insert / Sweep / Sweep Along A Guide** then select the second sketch for the section and the first sketch for the drive curve.

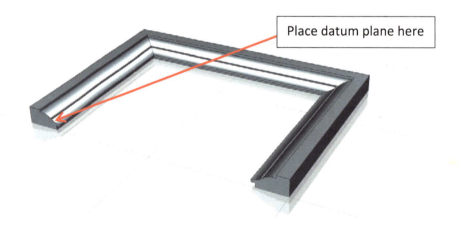

Place datum plane here

Next place a datum plane on the face shown with offset set to zero. Use **Insert / Datum/Point / Datum Plane** and use the inferred method. Simply select the flat plane and make sure the offset is set to zero.

Once you have created the datum plane, mirror the body about it and unite the two pieces together.

Next assemble the two models into a new part called **Glass Door Assembly**.

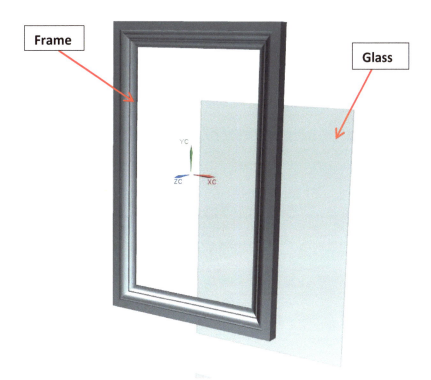

Frame

Glass

Within the assembly part file, create expressions that will be used to control both parts. Use **Tools / Expression** and enter **length=20**, **width=12** and **thickness=.25**. These are the expressions that you will now link to from the other components. The expression editor in the assembly part file should show up as depicted in the diagram that follows:

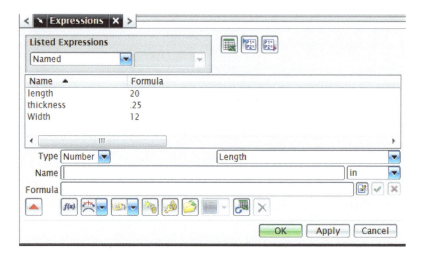

Next, create an interpart expression inside the glass part that references the assembly part. To do this, make sure that **Glass** is the work part. Then select **Tools / Expression** and click on the **l** dimension that you created earlier. Once **l** is loaded into the **Name** box in the editor, select the Interpart link icon.

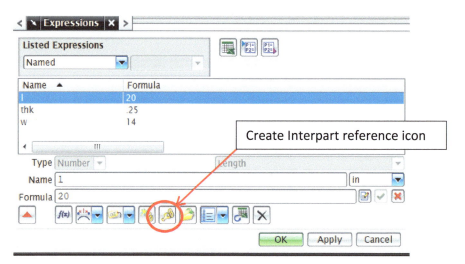

Create Interpart reference icon

The next menu that appears allows you to select the part file to which you will link.

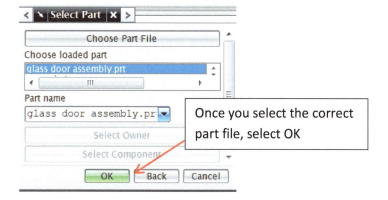

Once you select the correct part file, select OK

Navigate to the name of the assembly, which in this case is **glass door assembly.prt** and select **OK**. The next menu that appears is the **Create Interpart Reference** menu. This menu allows you to select the expression inside of the assembly that will link to the "**L**" expression in the glass component. The menu will appear as shown below:

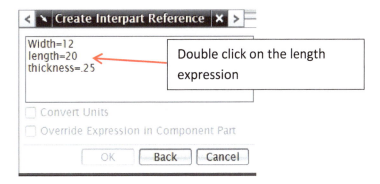

Once you double click *(or select the expression and press **OK**)*, the link will be complete. This should look as shown below:

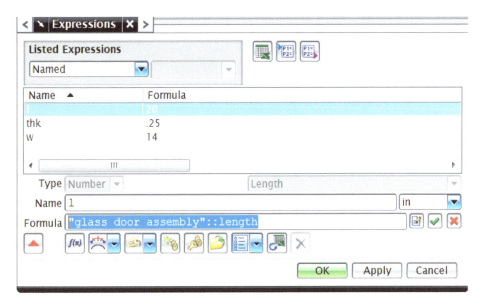

Repeat the process for **thk** and **w**. The **w** should equal "**glass door assembly**"::**width** and **thk** will equal "**glass door assembly**"::**thk**. You can make these links manually by typing in the part name from which the link will be defined in between quotes, followed by two colons, followed by the name of the expression to which you want to link. You can also copy and paste the formula from one expression to another . (Use the little green checkbox button and the little red X button to the right of the Formula input field to complete or cancel formula entry and switch to another expression.).

The next step is to link the expression of the frame part to the assembly. Make the frame the work part and navigate to **Tools / Expression.** First link "**q**" which is half the length of the frame and link it to the "**length**" variable in frame. Make sure you divide it by 2. It should appear as shown in the following figure:

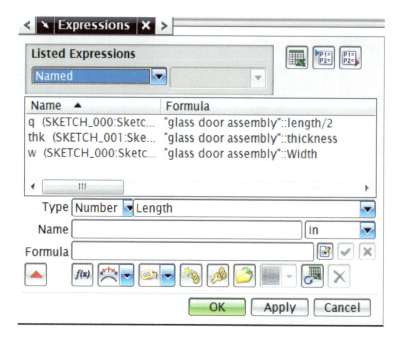

Now that you have both components linked, use Assembly Constraints to nest the glass inside of the frame.

Then change the expression in the assembly part file so length is equal to **40** and width is equal to **14**. Both components will immediately change shape:

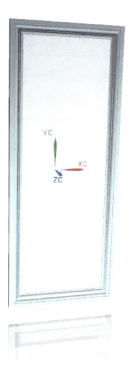

This window assembly is an example of a "**top down**" design, where expressions created in subassemblies or components look up to the parent assembly for the expression values. This can be an extremely powerful technique used in building modular parametric designs.

End of Exercise

11. Spreadsheet Edit

The spreadsheet edit function in the expressions language allows you to make modeling changes via the spreadsheet. This means you are able to access the awesome power of a spread sheet to perform edits that might be a bit too complex to get done efficiently in the conventional way. For example suppose you had a model of a pressure vessel cover. You can enter the **Spreadsheet Edit** function and at a glance you can see all the expressions that are pertinent to the model.

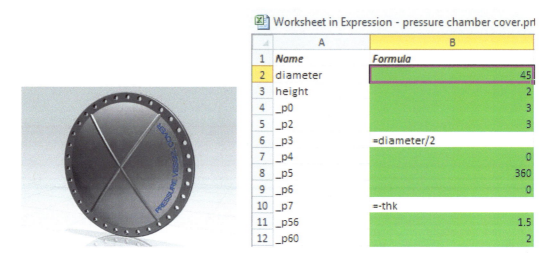

When a model change is desired, one can re-enter the spreadsheet and change the diameter dimension from 45 to 80 inches. Next navigate within the actual spreadsheet to the Add-ins button. Exit the spreadsheet and refresh the expression editor. The change will then be made to the part.

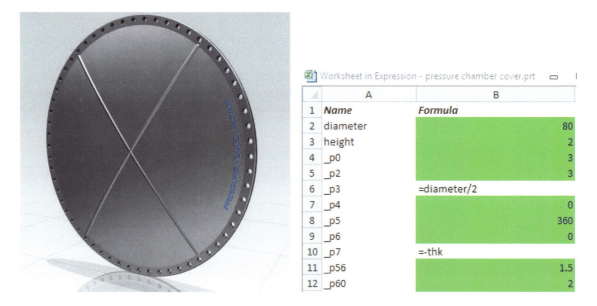

Exercise 11.1 Spreadsheet Edit

In this exercise you will practice using a spreadsheet to modify the expression values of the model shown below.

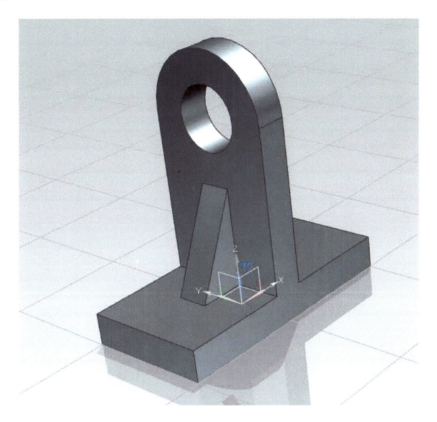

The first step is to create the following expressions list:

a	6	6	in	Num...
d	1.5	1.5	in	Num...
l	6	6	in	Num...
thk	.75	0.75	in	Num...
w	3	3	in	Num...

Next create the model shown above using the newly created expressions shown in the following sketches. First, create the sketch that is shown below:

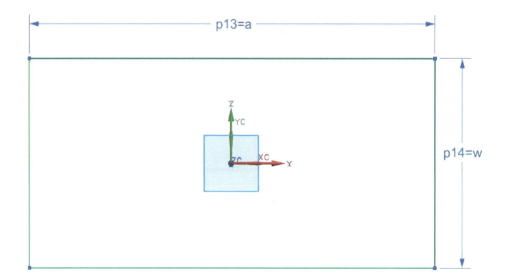

On an orthogonal plane, create the next sketch, and then extrude the first sketch to a value of **thk** as shown below.

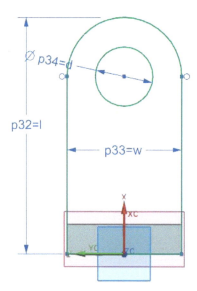

Next extrude the second sketch to a value of **thk/2** using the "**Symmetric Value**" switch in the extrude menu. Also create the little triangular sketches shown below on a center datum plane, and extrude them with the symmetric value to **thk/2.**

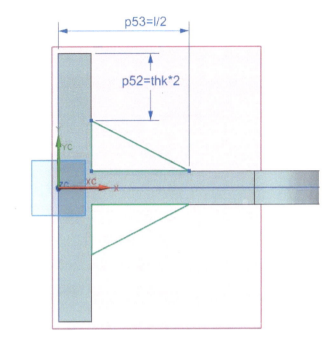

Using spreadsheet editing within the expressions editor, export your expressions to a spreadsheet for editing.

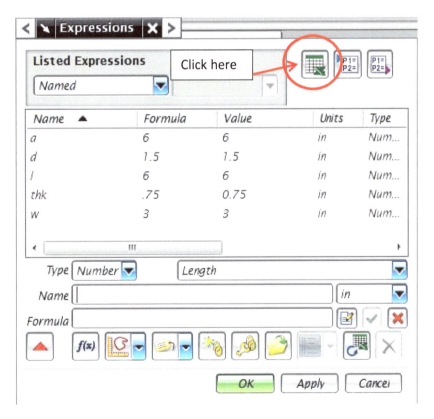

Once you have clicked the icon the expressions you've created, as well as all the other automatically generated expressions are sent to a spreadsheet in excel as shown in the diagram to follow.

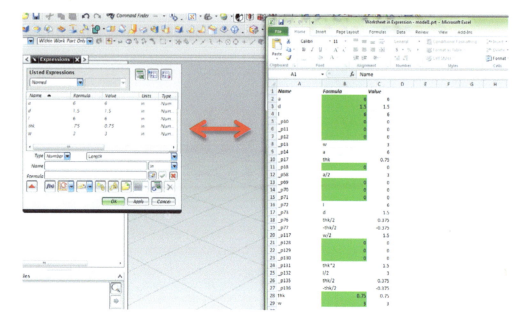

From within Excel change the values as shown below:

- L = 8
- W = 2.5
- A = 5
- THK = 0.5
- D = 1

Finally, send the values back to NX by clicking "**Update Expressions**" in the Add-Ins menu found in the top of the Expressions dialog.

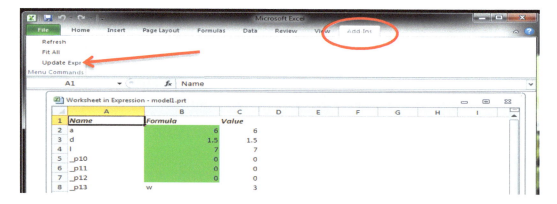

The result will be a new shape for the product.

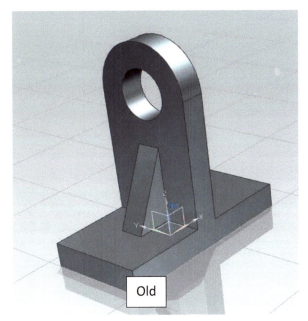

Old

New

End of Exercise

12. Refresh Values from Spreadsheet

To control model expressions with an external spreadsheet you can use the "**Refresh Values from External Spreadsheet**" function in the expressions editor.

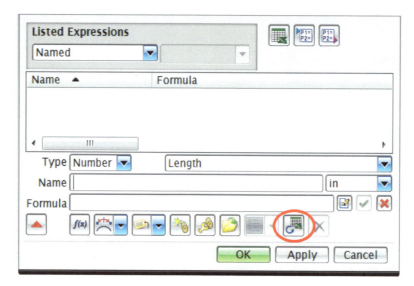

This enables you to link the geometry of a part to some pre-existing spreadsheet that may have all sorts of complex calculations going on in the background. The spreadsheet can be opened or closed as long as the path name is clear. For this function to work you must have the appropriate spreadsheet functions in your expression formula, namely "**ug_cell_read**". An example on how to use this function is shown below:

ug_cell_read("path name to file","cell in file")

NX has numerous built in functions for doing lookups within tables of spreadsheet data like retrieving entire ranges of numbers into a List expression.

The possibilities are as endless as the capabilities in the spreadsheet themselves. This function allows you to create complex modeling changes without even having NX open at the time. For example, imagine you have created a part file of a gear. The main variables driving the geometry might be number of teeth, tooth width, pressure angle and gear width. Next you create a spreadsheet named gear with values in specific cells that reflect those important values. Then you link all the important values of the model part file to the spreadsheet.

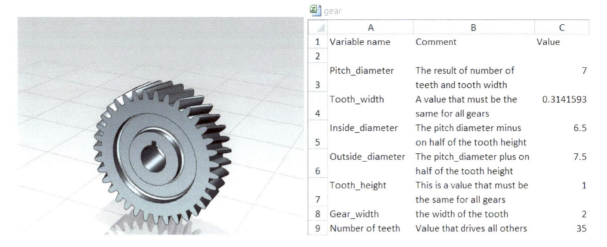

	A	B	C
1	Variable name	Comment	Value
2			
3	Pitch_diameter	The result of number of teeth and tooth width	7
4	Tooth_width	A value that must be the same for all gears	0.3141593
5	Inside_diameter	The pitch diameter minus on half of the tooth height	6.5
6	Outside_diameter	The pitch_diameter plus on half of the tooth height	7.5
7	Tooth_height	This is a value that must be the same for all gears	1
8	Gear_width	the width of the tooth	2
9	Number of teeth	Value that drives all others	35

Once you have everything that is important to drive the geometry linked to the spreadsheet you simply change the values in the spreadsheet and save them. Finally you go back into the NX part file, enter the Expressions editor and select "Refresh Values from Spreadsheet". NX will navigate to where ever the spreadsheet lives on the operating system, open Excel, and read the values. That's pretty cool!

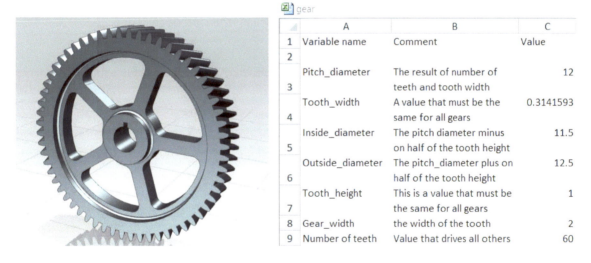

	A	B	C
1	Variable name	Comment	Value
2			
3	Pitch_diameter	The result of number of teeth and tooth width	12
4	Tooth_width	A value that must be the same for all gears	0.3141593
5	Inside_diameter	The pitch diameter minus on half of the tooth height	11.5
6	Outside_diameter	The pitch_diameter plus on half of the tooth height	12.5
7	Tooth_height	This is a value that must be the same for all gears	1
8	Gear_width	the width of the tooth	2
9	Number of teeth	Value that drives all others	60

The Expressions dialog editor will show the link to the spreadsheet in the formula column as shown in the following figure:

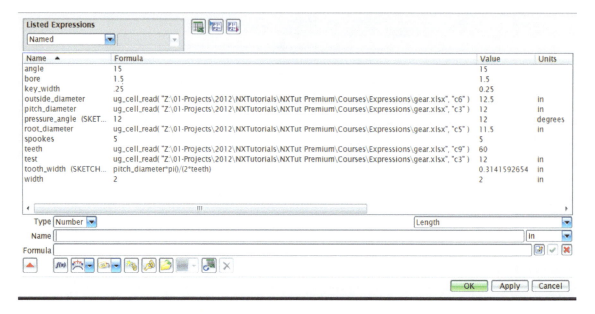

Note: *This function is very powerful yet must be used with great care. Like anything else that is powerful it comes with a bit of a risk. Since the spreadsheet contains much of the logic that defines and drives the part geometry you must be careful not to let the NX file and the spreadsheet file become separated. Also, it may be confusing to a user who happens to use the model. If they don't know how the technique works they may go into the file and accidentally break the links.*

The latest versions of NX have a new ability to lock an expression formula to reduce this kind of inadvertent damage to important expressions. This "lock formula" command can be applied from the MB3 menu in the Expressions dialog. While the formula is locked, an expression continues to update exactly as before, but the expression formula is protected from being changed without a deliberate unlocking action.

It is the strong opinion of the author that problems like these are best avoided by ensuring everyone who will be working with the files is highly CAD-literate. There is no substitute for a creative and empowered user who's been given the time to learn and practice all this stuff.

Exercise 12.1: Refresh Values from Spreadsheet

In this exercise you will learn how to create a component that is controlled by variables in a spreadsheet. The example is that of a small nose cone.

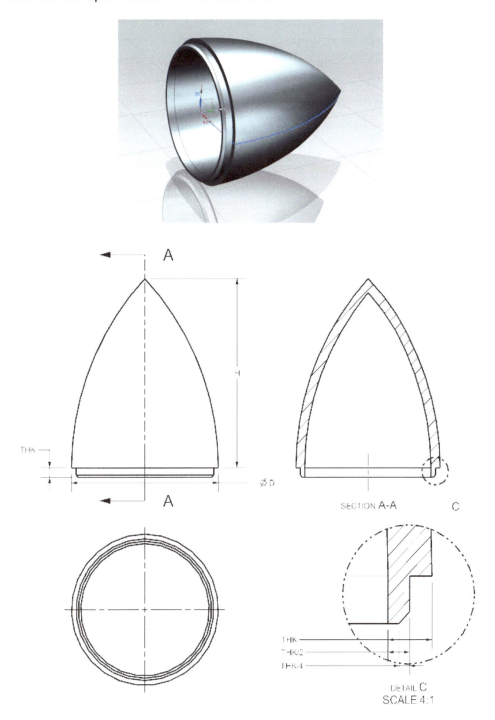

To proceed, create an excel spreadsheet that contains the following variables in columns shown below:

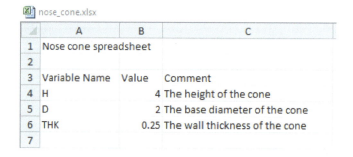

	A	B	C
1	Nose cone spreadsheet		
2			
3	Variable Name	Value	Comment
4	H	4	The height of the cone
5	D	2	The base diameter of the cone
6	THK	0.25	The wall thickness of the cone
7			

Once you have created the spreadsheet, be sure to save it on the desktop as "nose_cone.xls".

Once the spreadsheet is complete and saved enter NX and create a sketch that is shown below:

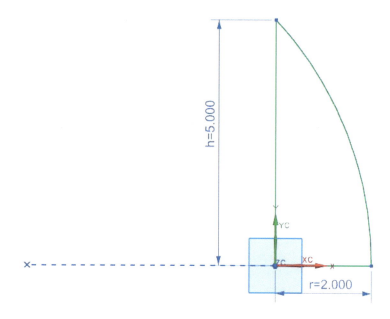

Notice that the sketch dimensions have been edited to reflect two dimensions "h" and "r". The next step is to revolve the sketch as shown below:

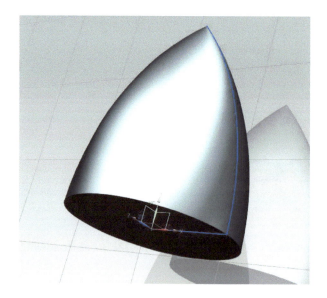

The next thing to do is to shell the revolve body removing the bottom face. As you create the shell enter in "**THK=.25**" into the thickness field. This way you will simultaneously create the **THK** expression and shell the body.

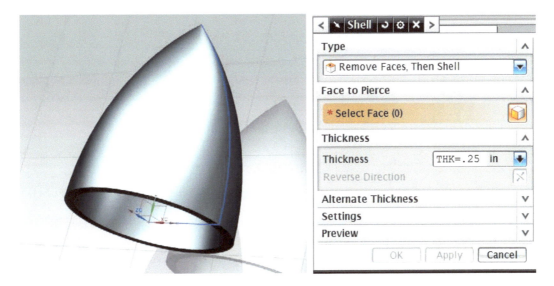

Once you have a shelled body, extrude the inside edge downward with a two sided offset. The extrude distance will be **THK** and the offset will be **0** and **THK/2**. Unite the extrude and create a chamfer on the edge that is set equal to **THK/4**.

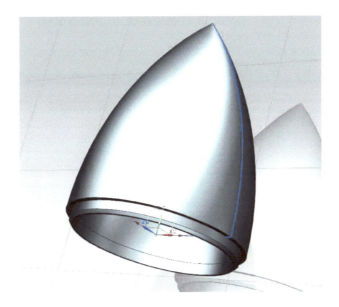

Now to link the model to the spreadsheet. Open the expression editor and find the **H** expession that you creted while in the sketcher. Click on the the "**H**" variable and it will apear in the "**Name**" bar.

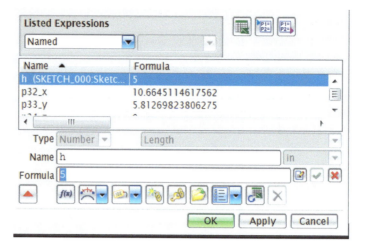

Once you have the **H** formula loaded into the Name and Formula fields, press the "**Functions**" button in the lower left corner of the main Expressions dialog:

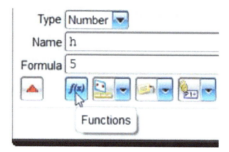

From here, choose "Spreadsheet" from the list of function categories (and note that there is a great variety of out-of-the-box functions available.):

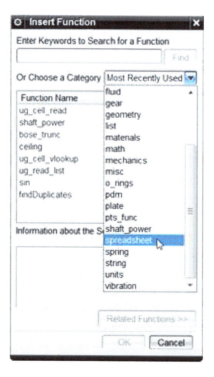

Choose "**ug_cell_read**" from the list of out-of-the-box functions, and click the **OK** button.

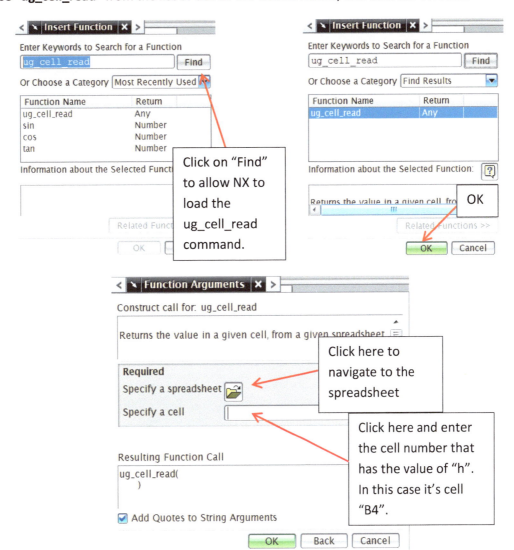

The "**Functions Arguments**" menu allows you to navigate to the spreadsheet file and input the cell of the reference that is supposed to contol the expesssion. Once you've input the cell reference and selected **OK** you will return directly to the main Expressions dialog, and the function will have been populated in the **Formula** field like this:

Do the same for the other expressions. Make sure you divide the diameter by 2 when linking it to **r** of the sketch. When you have linked the three expressions H, D and THK, your expressions should appear as shown in the following figure:

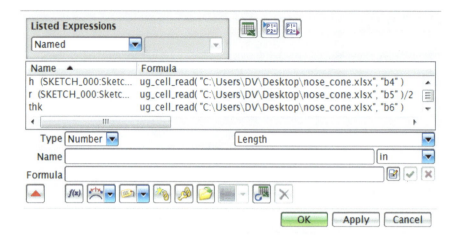

Now that you have all the expressions linked, set the values in your spreadsheet to those shown below:

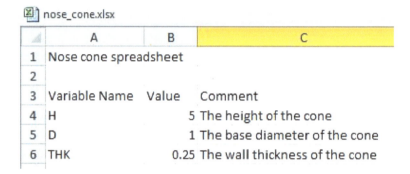

Now save the spreadsheet by selecting **File > Save** in Excel mode. Once done you are ready to perform the **Refresh Values from Spreadsheet** command whose result should appear as shown below:

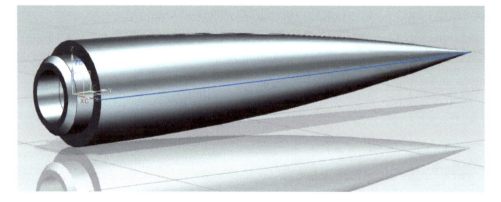

End of Exercise

13. Using Requirement Checks with Expressions

There are many types of component geometries that have specific size and shape requirements that cannot be emulated with numbers that vary linearly. For example, the holes in a pressure vessel cover may vary according to the size of bolts that will be used to hold it on. The size of the bolts will match standard sizes and therefore will not vary linearly.

Requirement Checks are rules and flags you can set on an expression to describe a desired range of values for an expression. This range can be expressed using greater than or less than operators, equal or not equal operators, or an explicit set of desired values. This allows you to set some external logic on an expression to ensure that value used to drive a model (or a value that is measured or calculated from the model) is limited to what is desirable – and to warn a user if it is not.

In the following model a plate of sheet metal is bent in the way shown. It is a device that is meant for law enforcement agencies for situations where there is a high speed car chase. The idea is for an officer in pursuit of a get-away car to drive ahead and throw a bunch of these devices out of the window to shred the tires of the get-away car. No matter which way they land they will be capable of puncturing the tires. The question is from what gauge material they should be constructed?

In the expressions editor the expressions Requirement Checks button is located toward the bottom right.

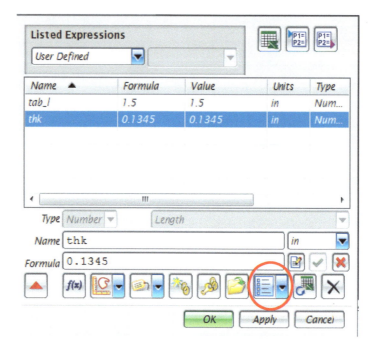

By clicking this button while having the targeted expression highlighted you are presented with a dialog in which you will define the requirement. Note that you will describe the "positive" or "desired" condition here, as opposed to the failure condition.

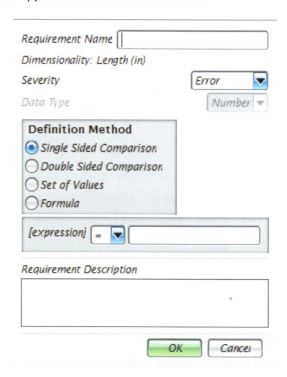

From within the expressions requirement window a name must be specified for the requirement. A "**Severity**" can be chosen from the following:

- Error
- Warning
- Information

The "**Definition Method**" allows you to choose the logic used to evaluate the expression against the requirement. A single sided comparison is virtually the same as a basic if statement e.g. if x > y. Double sided comparison allows you to specify a double-ended range within which the expression value must fall. The set of values option allows the user to tell NX that the target expression must exactly match one of the listed values. These values can be listed on separate lines or separated by semicolons. The formula option allows the user to specify a more advanced logical operation, as opposed to using one of the more basic standard options.

Note: *When writing a Requirement formula, use the [expression] syntax exactly as you see it appear in the other pre-canned options above. In other words, just like the Single-Sided Expression entry displays this:*

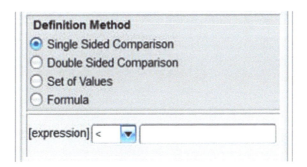

...you should use the [expression] syntax like this to enter a more complex formula:

(This one means, "The target expression must be greater than zero AND less than or equal to six, OR the target expression must be equal to the expression "size".)

Finally the user can specify a description for the requirement, letting other users know quickly what the requirement is for, and any other useful data.

For the model shown above different gauges of sheet metal will be needed for manufacturing, thus we want to make sure that the thickness expression matches the standard sheet metal gauge thicknesses.

Gauge (ga)	Standard Steel Thickness (inches)	Galvanized Steel Thickness (inches)	Aluminum Thickness (inches)
3	0.2391		0.2294
4	0.2242		0.2043
5	0.2092		0.1819
6	0.1943		0.1620
7	0.1793		0.1443
8	0.1644		0.1285
9	0.1495	0.1532	0.1144
10	0.1345	0.1382	0.1019
11	0.1196	0.1233	0.0907
12	0.1046	0.1084	0.0808
13	0.0897	0.0934	0.0720
14	0.0747	0.0785	0.0641
15	0.0673	0.0710	0.0571
16	0.0598	0.0635	0.0508
17	0.0538	0.0575	0.0453
18	0.0478	0.0516	0.0403

The requirement to be set on the thickness expression should be that the thickness has to match 16, 12, or 10 gauge sheet metal. For this requirement the "**Set of Values**" option will be chosen. . The valid values field can be populated as shown below:

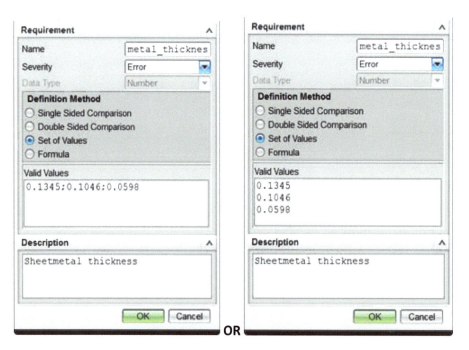

OR

By trying to apply a value that was not specified in the rule set for sheet metal thickness, an error is generated in NX within the expressions editor.

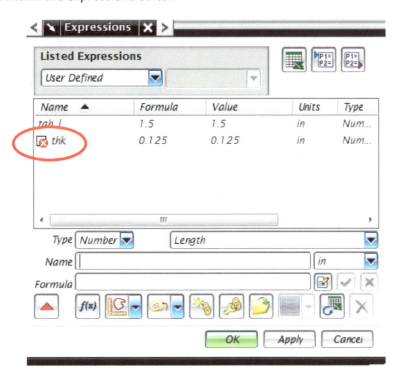

This notifies the user that something is wrong with the model and needs to be corrected.

Requirements Validation:

To check whether a model passes the requirements quickly without having to sort through the expressions editor there is another useful informational tool in NX called Requirements Validation.

There are two ways to get to Requirements Validation, One is to navigate to the menu under **Analysis / Requirements Validation**, and the second way is through the resource bar (*on the left, by default*) from within the **HD3D Tools** tab.

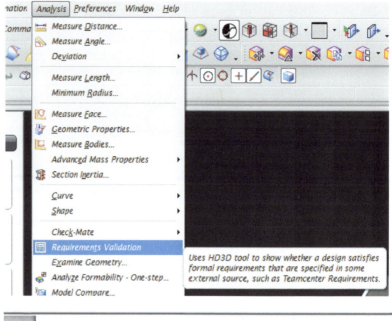

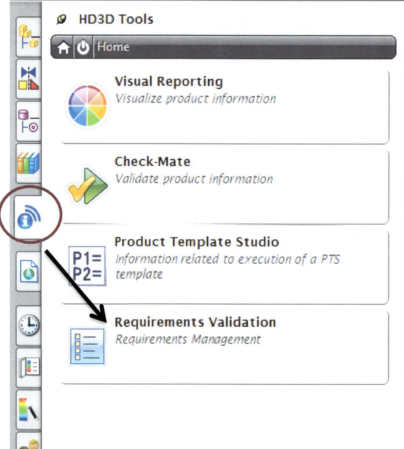

From the Requirements Validation tool a user can immediately see all Requirements that have been specified for the part (or for all parts in your NX session) and the pass/fail/warning/info state of all Requirement Checks that compare expressions against those requirements.

Note: With the judicious use of Requirement Checks, this Requirements Validation tool can be a powerful view into the "health" of a complex parametric model.

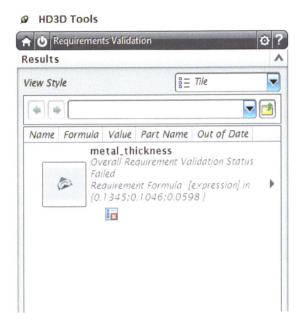

As you can see in the previous figure metal_thickness failed the overall requirement. If the user double clicks on the requirement NX gives a visual display of what part of the model this expression affects. *(If the expression was created by a modeling feature, then we use that feature geometry to display the HD3D tag in the graphics area. If the expression is a user-defined expression, or if you just don't love where the tag is coming up, you can choose to attach the tag to any other visible model geometry as well.)*

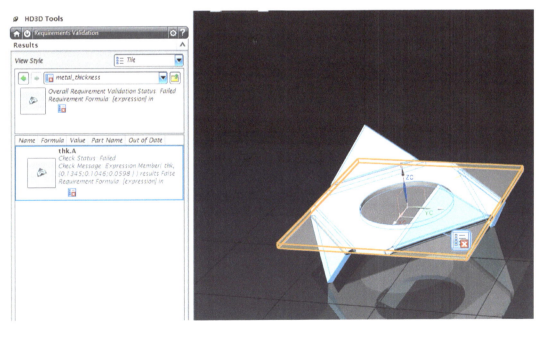

If the user double clicks on the error icon displayed over the model, a detailed report will show containing more information on what failed.

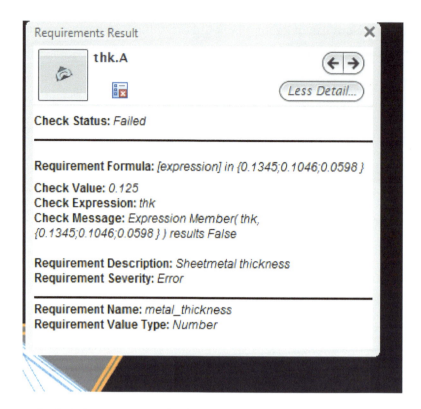

By right clicking on the failed requirement (*either in the HD3D tool or on the HD3D tag in the graphics area*) a pop-up menu will display presenting several options for the user to correct the problem. The user can go back into the expression editor from here or the user can refine the requirement as well as delete the requirement check entirely.

Exercise 13.1 Using Requirement Checks with Expressions

In this exercise you will create a model of an aircraft bracket that has a requirement that the weight does not exceed a certain value. To proceed you must first create a model of the bracket, assign a material to it, create a measurement expression that captures the weight, then create the requirement check.

First create the expression that will control the bracket h=7, w=2, hole=1, leg=2, thk=.5

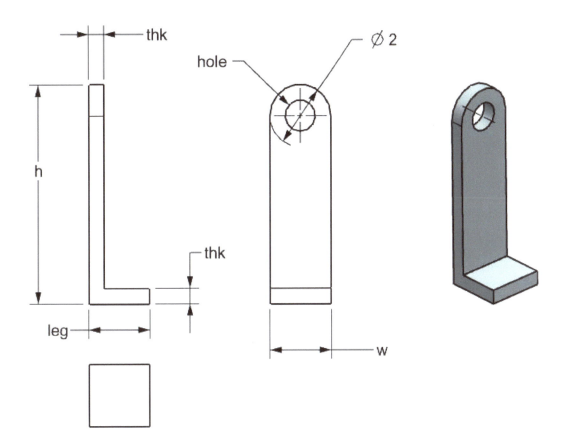

Create the model in such a way that when you change the value of **h**, **thk**, **w** and **leg** the bracket changes appropriately.

To assign the density use **Tools / Materials / Assign Materials** and choose **Aluminum 6061**. Then select the material and choose apply.

Next select **Tools / Expression / Measure Bodies** select the solid and choose OK to create the set of body measurement expressions. One of these will be for the weight The value should be about 0.77lbs. The requirement that you will create will be "The weight should be less than or equal to 2 lbs." When the weight is greater than 2 we will want NX to issue an error to alert the user.

Note: *Again, remember that we will describe the "positive" or "desired" condition in the Requirement, and not the error condition.*

To proceed you highlight the expression for the force and click on "**New Requirements**"

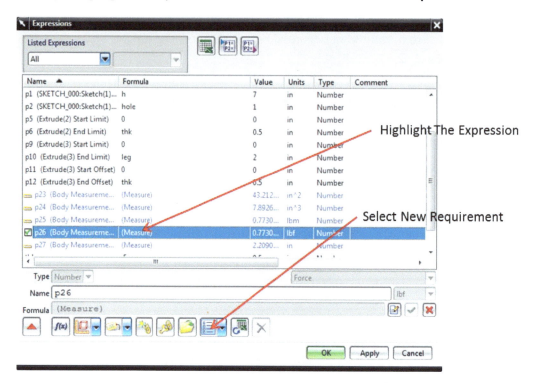

A dialog will appear in which you will create the requirement. You may name it, choose the definition method, choose the severity, input a description and set its operators.

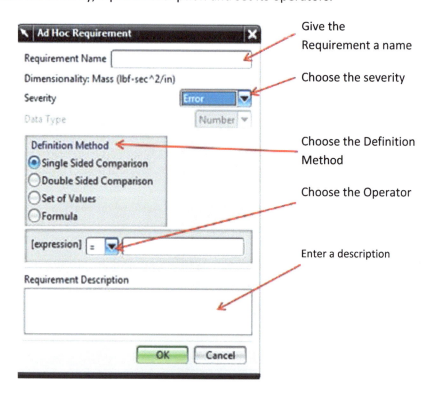

In this example use the following settings:

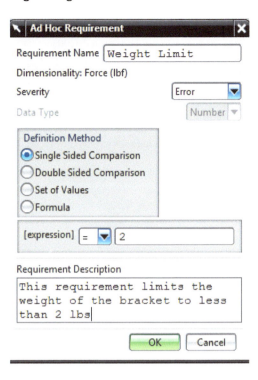

Once you have the requirements defined, Select **OK** and the requirement (*and an associated Requirement Check*) will be created.

Now to test it out — edit expression **w** to equal 7. In response, the weight of the solid should climb to about **2.6** lbs. An indicator will appear on the expression being checked as shown below:

Now that you have violated the requirement you can also view it more easily in the Requirements validation **HD3D** tool. Choose the HD3D tab ( ) from the resource bar. The **HD3D** Tools menu will appear:

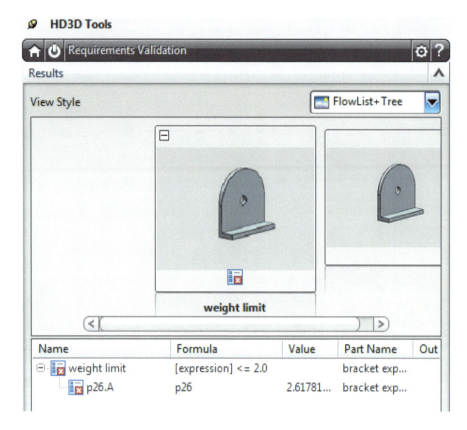

In the main graphics window, a small HD3D tag should be visible on the 3D model:

End of exercise

14. Part Families

Once you are adept at using the expression editor and the spreadsheet you can easily grasp the concept of "**Part Families**". Part families in NX are extremely useful because they enable you to create the type of component that comes in many sizes such as a fastener or a prosthetic, and then organize the variant models using a spreadsheet. For example, consider the simplified fastener below. The length is controlled by a variable called "**shaft_length**", the diameter of the shaft controlled by "**shaft_dia**", the thickness of the head of the fastener controlled by "**head_thk**", and the diameter of the head is controlled by "**head_dia**". The model is made up of a cylinder and a boss.

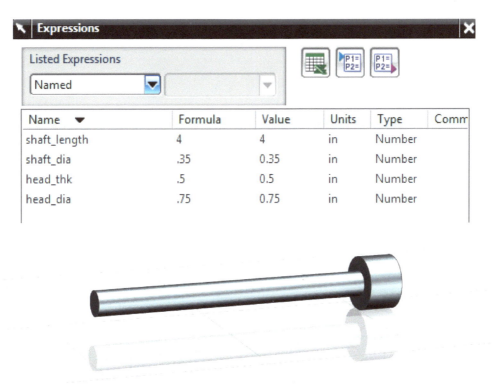

The objective is to create a number of fasteners with the same build but with varying dimensions. To that end the next step is to use the **Part Families** function. (**Tools > Part Families**)

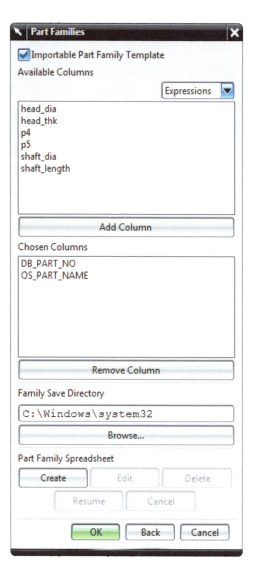

Once there, you should click in the "**Browse**" box and select a suitable location where all the family members will be placed. When done, you may select the columns that you want to be part of the spreadsheet. As you may notice in the example there are expressions for P4 and P5 that don't need to be part of the spreadsheet. When you have chosen all the expressions that you want to include in the spreadsheet you select "**Create**" and you are taken into the spreadsheet function.

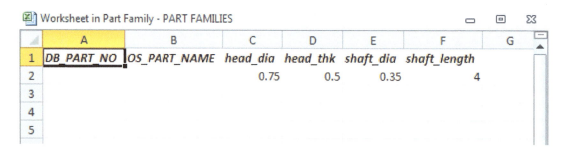

Next you enter all the information that the system will use to make new part files or part family members.

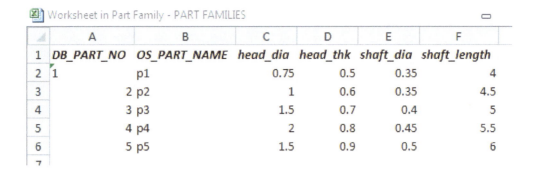

When you create all the parts with the create parts function they all go to the "**Family Save Directory**" specified back on the **Part Families** dialog (the one where you selected columns for the spreadsheet.).

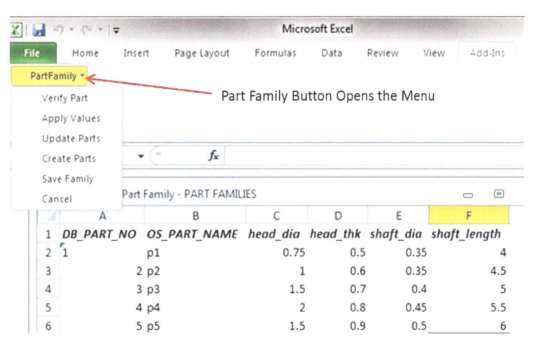

Part Family Button Opens the Menu

When you use a part family in an assembly, an extra menu appears that allows you to choose which member of the family (template) you will be using. The diagram that follows shows the menu.

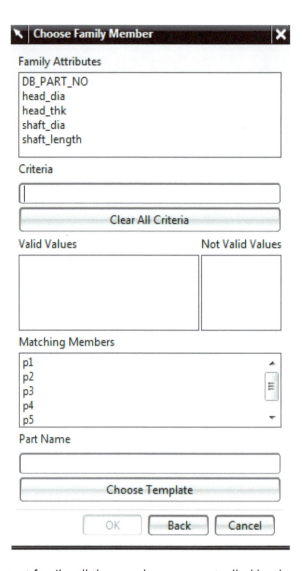

Choose Family Member

Family Attributes

```
DB_PART_NO
head_dia
head_thk
shaft_dia
shaft_length
```

Criteria

Clear All Criteria

Valid Values | Not Valid Values

Matching Members

```
p1
p2
p3
p4
p5
```

Part Name

Choose Template

OK | Back | Cancel

Once you have created a part family, all the members are controlled by the main part file (template) that was used to generate them. If you desire to make changes to all the members of the family, you can make a change to the original part then propagate the changes out to all the members by going back to the part family spreadsheet and choosing "**Add-Ins / Part Family/ Update Parts**".

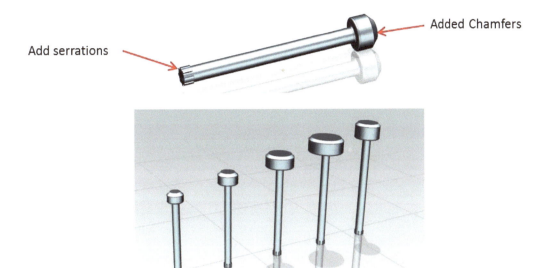

Add serrations → / ← Added Chamfers

Another extremely powerful aspect of part families is the ability to have assembly part files automatically select part family members based on a set of rules that you create using the standard mathematical operators listed below: Note that in the case of "=" you need two equal signs and in the case of "&" you need two ampersand signs which means "**and**".

<   means less than

<=   means less than or equal to

==   means equal to

!=   means not equal to

>   means greater than

&&   means and. For example if I wanted X to be equal to 5 if A equals 3 and B equals 5.

|| means or. This one is tricky. It's the vertical bar that you get by pressing shift back
slash

These operators are used to create criteria that are written in code similar to the programming language c++. A more detailed explanation will be shown in the example to follow. An example of when to use part family members chosen by expression is that of a hatchway. Imagine you had a part file called door. The component was built into an assembly called hatchway which included the frame and the door. Both the frame and the door came in a variety of diameters and thicknesses. You could then write a criteria statement that said "automatically choose the door part family member that fit the frame based on the frame diameter and thickness". You would create a part family for the door and a parametric model of the frame that limited the diameter and thickness to those values that fit the various doors.

Exercise 14.1: Part Families

In this exercise you will practice the part family function using a small revolved shape as shown below:

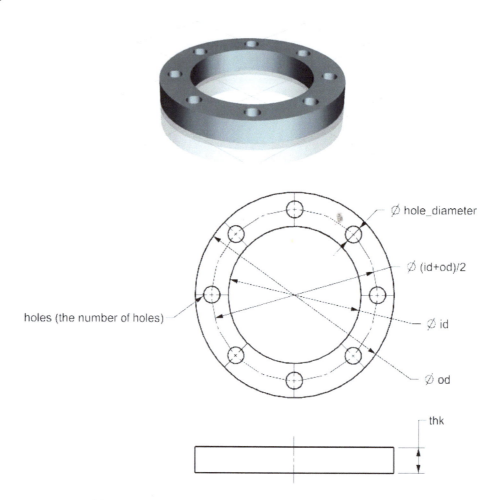

First, open a new part file and create the expressions in the editor shown below.

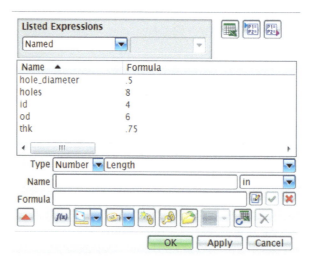

Next create a model with the dimensions shown above.

Once you have created the model, select **Tools / Part Families.** The menu that appears allows you to select the expressions that you will use to manipulate the part family. You will select the expression and select the "**Add Column**" button. Add the **hole_diameter**, **holes**, **id,od** and **thk** expressions.

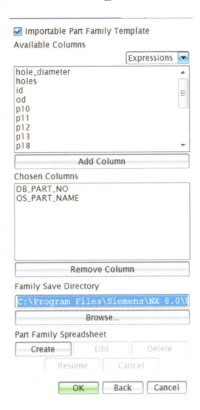

Also, select the **Browse** button and input a more suitable location for all the parts that you will create.

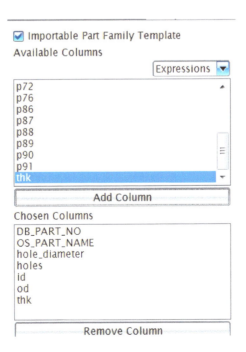

Next create an entry in the table for the existence of the hole feature. This can be accomplished by clicking on the down arrow by the box that says **Expressions** and changing it to **Features**.

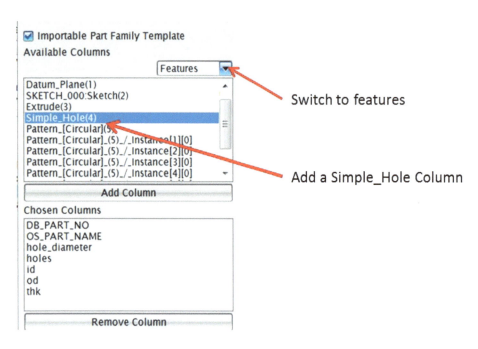

Once you have added the **Simple Hole** column you may select **OK** and a spreadsheet will be created. You can fill in the columns as shown below to create various models.

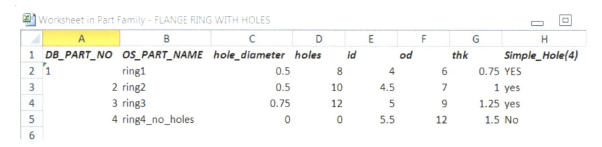

	A	B	C	D	E	F	G	H
1	DB_PART_NO	OS_PART_NAME	hole_diameter	holes	id	od	thk	Simple_Hole(4)
2	1	ring1	0.5	8	4	6	0.75	YES
3	2	ring2	0.5	10	4.5	7	1	yes
4	3	ring3	0.75	12	5	9	1.25	yes
5	4	ring4_no_holes	0	0	5.5	12	1.5	No
6								

Note: *Upper/lower case is not significant in the "Simple Hole" column above. Any combination will work, as long as you've used the right letters. Also note that "no" is the real keyword here. Anything other than "no/No/nO/NO" will be interpreted as a "yes". Even "True" and "False" are both treated as a "yes" here.*

Once you are done filling in all the columns you can select one of the cells and use the **Verify Part** command in the Add-Ins tab to ensure that the numbers that you've input are valid. In the example below cell A5 is highlighted and the resulting solid is shown.

Once you are satisfied that all the inputs are correct, you may highlight all rows in the part family (in this case, rows 2 through 5) and use the **Create Parts** command in the **Add-Ins** tab to generate all of these parts on your hard drive. The information window will appear and give you confirmation that all the parts that are commensurate with all the values you placed in the spreadsheet have been created.

```
i  Information
File   Edit
Creating member parts for family...
Created member ring1
Created member ring2
Created member ring3
Created member ring4_no_holes
```

Once you have created all the parts, you may open up a new assembly and assemble each member. When you select the main part file you will receive a menu that will allow you to select the specific part family member that you desire.

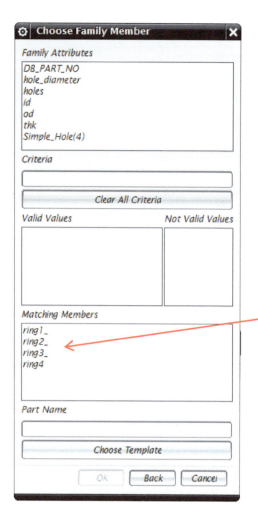

Choose part family member

End of Exercise

Exercise 14.2: Selecting a Part Family Member using an Expression

In this exercise you will use an expression at the assembly level to select a fastener part family member (*and then be able to automatically replace it*) as a design changes parametrically. This process is a bit complex so here is an over view of the basic steps:

1. Create an assembly with a measurement expression for some critical dimension that will dictate the choice of family members. In this example you will have two plates with a hole in each. Based on the thickness of the plates a fastener of the correct length will be selected.
2. Create a family table with a fastener that has various lengths.
3. Bring the fastener into the assembly and perform the special magic that will tell the family part which member to select. The special magic is "**code**" that you insert into the Criteria field of the "**Choose Family Member**" menu.
4. Change the thickness of one or both of the plates then perform a "**Part Family Update**" and the part family member selection will be made and the part will be replaced.

First, you'll need an assembly into which you will insert your fastener. For the sake of simplicity create the assembly shown below. It doesn't matter what name you give the assembly or the components, however, please create a measurement expression called "**h**" from the bottom of the bottom plate to the top of the top plate. This will dictate the length of the fastener.

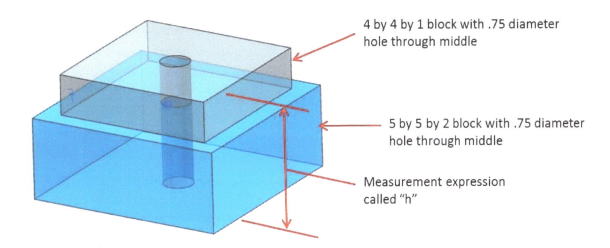

4 by 4 by 1 block with .75 diameter hole through middle

5 by 5 by 2 block with .75 diameter hole through middle

Measurement expression called "h"

Next create a part family fastener with four members of various lengths. Start by creating a part file called fastener with a 1 inch diameter head that is .5 thick and a boss below it that is .7 in diameter and 4 inches in length. In the expression editor, label the expression that controls the length of the boss to "**Length**".

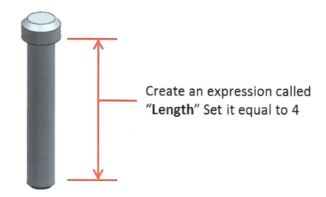

Create an expression called
"**Length**" Set it equal to 4

Once you've created the component, create a part family spreadsheet out of it. Make only four members. Simply name them P1, p2, p3 and p4. Give them lengths that begin at 4 and go up by 1 inch increments as shown below.

Make a very simple part family

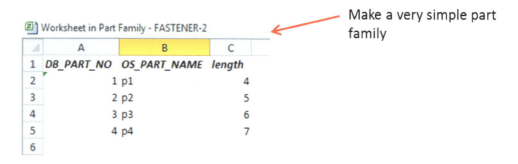

Now you are ready to bring the part family member into the assembly. As you do this, you will be prompted for the special "**code**" that allows the assembly to automatically choose the part family member. Choose **Assemblies/Components/Add components** and select the fastener. Use **By Constraints** for the positioning method and select **OK**. You will get the following menu:

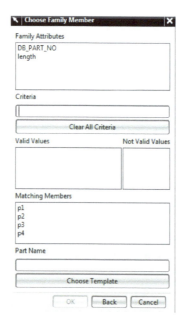

Next select "**Length**" from the Family Attributes panel

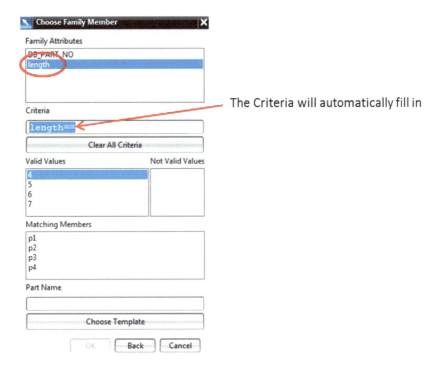

The Criteria will automatically fill in

Next, set **length** that appears in the Criteria window to equal the conditional expression that will select the correct fastener family member. The expression is based on "**h**" (the measurement expression that automatically updates based on the combined thicknesses of the two plates).

The expression is input as "**(length>=h)&&(length<=h+1)**". Note: The logic of this expression is it will choose a family member whose length matches both of the conditions of being greater to or equal to h and less than or equal to h+1.

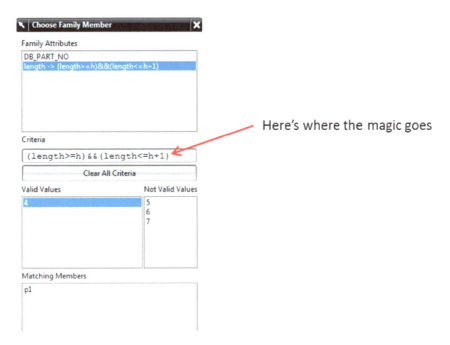

Here's where the magic goes

When you select OK, the appropriate part family member is selected and you can use assembly constraints to position it. In this case since the combined thickness of the two plates is three, the logical choice for the fastener is "p1", the family member with length set to 4.

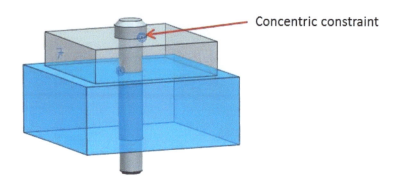

Concentric constraint

Now that the assembly is all together and the right criteria has been written, the fastener should automatically change when one or more of the plates gets thicker. To demonstrate, change the thickness of the top plate to 3.5.

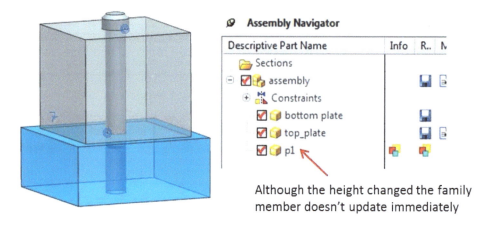

Although the height changed the family member doesn't update immediately

Finally you must give the assembly a push using the **Assemblies / Components / Part Family Update** command.

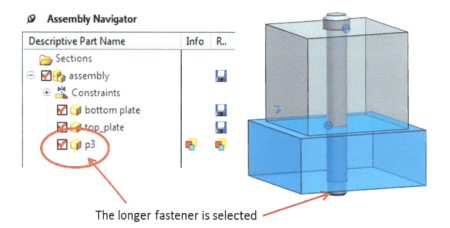

The longer fastener is selected

Also notice how NX creates a report that shows what happened. The highlighted line shown below reports to you that component p1 has been replaced by p3 with a family member selection criteria of "**(length>=h)&&(length<=h+1)**".

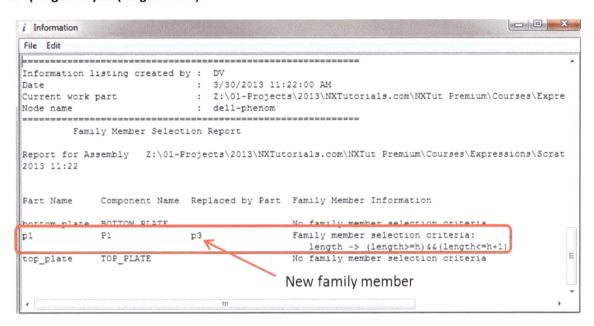

Next, make the plates such that none of the members are suitable for the given criteria. Make the thickness of the top plate 8 inches. When you select **Assemblies / Components / Part Family Update** no new member will be selected and you will receive a Family Member Selection Report similar to the one shown below. Notice there is no part family member listed in the "Replaced by Part" column:

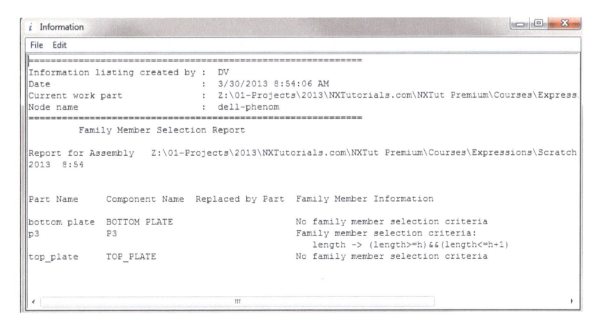

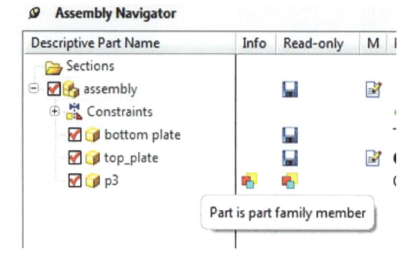

Note that both the Info column and the Read-only columns in the Assembly Navigator display a special icon for part family members. (Remember that part family members are created in a read-only state, and all changes must be made through the part family master part.)

Note: When the criteria are written in a way that enables more than one complying choice, NX will choose the first family member that appears in the spreadsheet.

End of Exercise

15. Spreadsheet Goal Seek

The Goal seek ability in the spreadsheet enables you to find the answers to geometric questions that are otherwise very difficult to answer. The water level in this vase is controlled by a variable called h.

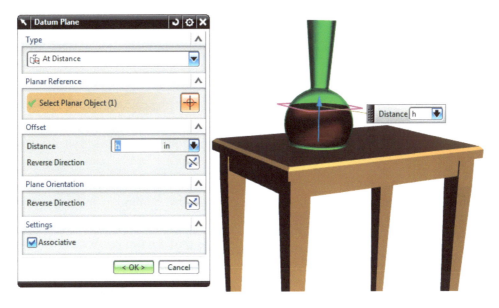

The volume of the liquid in the vase is represented by the crimson solid. The solid has been given a measurement expression that indicates the volume. When **h=6** the volume is **560.7** in^3. There's another expression that has been created called **v** which converts the volume into gallons (**v=volume_in_inches_cubed/231**). When **h=6** there are **2.43** gallons of liquid. When **h=4** there are **1.64 gallons**.

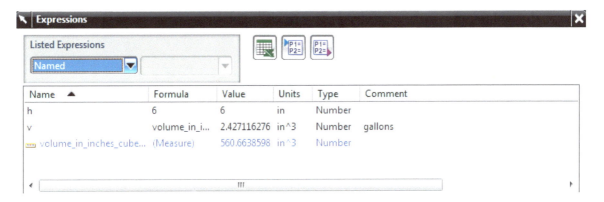

It is desired to create a graduation mark on the vase at the location where the liquid volume is exactly 2 gallons. The goal seek ability is used to find the exact **h** that will correspond to exactly **2** gallons. Sure – you could simply keep plugging in values for **h** until you find **v** equal to **2**. But using the goal seek you can have NX do it for you and this is especially useful when the geometric situation is very complex and non-linear.

To proceed, after having created the model and all the expressions, you simply access the spreadsheet. (**Tools / Spreadsheet**)

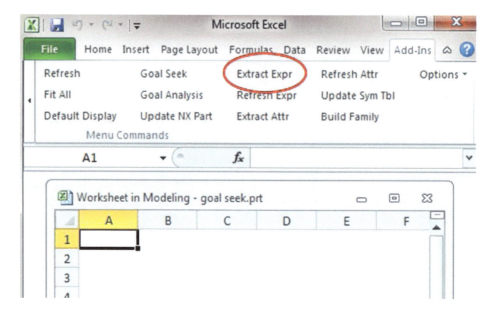

In a tab called "**Add-Ins**" you select the "**Extract Expressions**" command and it loads all the model expressions into the spreadsheet and gives contol of the model to the spreadsheet. All the expressions will be loaded and you may delete all those that are not necessary. The result is to have a spreadsheet that shows "**h**" and "**v**".

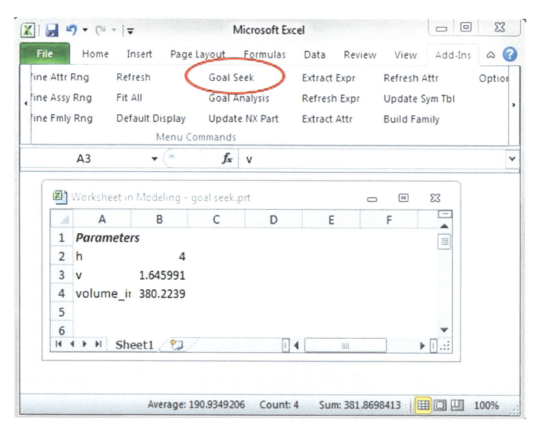

Now the fun begins. When you select "**Goal Seek**" you get a curious little menu:

When you fill out all the colums, and select **OK** the spreadsheet automatically makes educated guesses as to what **h** value will bring about the target value of your choice. In this particular case the variable cell is **B2**, the target cell is **B3**, the target value is **2** gallons, the lower bracket is **4** and the upper bracket is **6**. You can leave the tolerance at 1 times 10 to the minus 7. This is very accurate, and you can leave the maximum number of iterations at 20. This ensures that NX won't keep trying and trying all day if it can't find a solution. It's fun to watch the model change as the spreadsheet iterates.

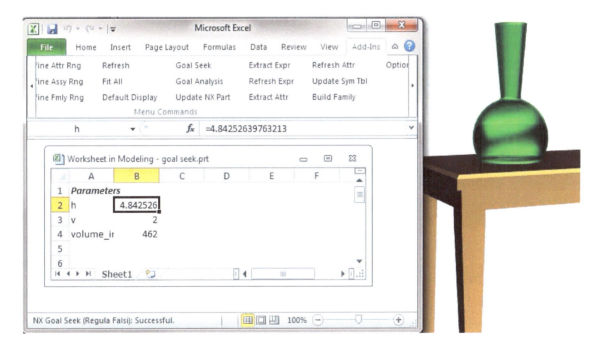

After the run in this example **h** was found to be **4.843**.

Exercise 15.1 Using Spreadsheet Goal Seek

In this example you will create a simple shape and use the goal seek to find the dimensions that will bring about the perfect weight. To begin, create the solid shown below by first creating a point. Use **Insert / Datum/ Point / point and type 0,0,5**. Then a sketch on the x-y plane. Then using **Insert / Mesh Surface / Through Curves.** Make sure that the "**Preserve Shape**" switch is turned on in settings.

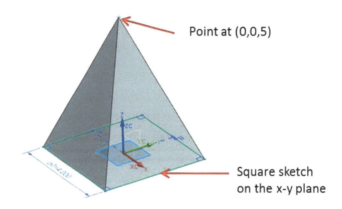

Point at (0,0,5)

Square sketch
on the x-y plane

Next, assign the material of aluminum 6061 to the model. Use **Tools / Materials / Assign Materials** and select "**Aluminum_6061**" then select the geometry and select **OK**.

Next Select **Tools / Expression**

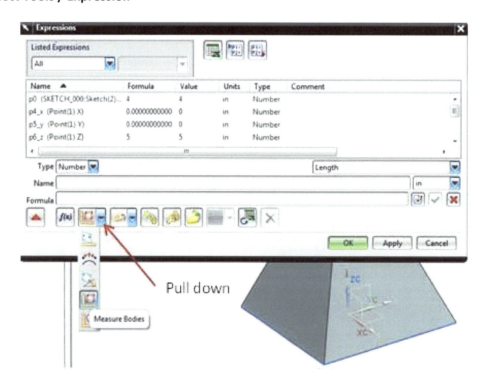

Pull down

Select **Measure Bodies** and select on the solid. The result should be a number of expressions. One of which will be the weight. You should get 2.61 lbs.

Now to perform the goal seek use **Tools Spreadsheet / Add-In tab / Extract Expressions**

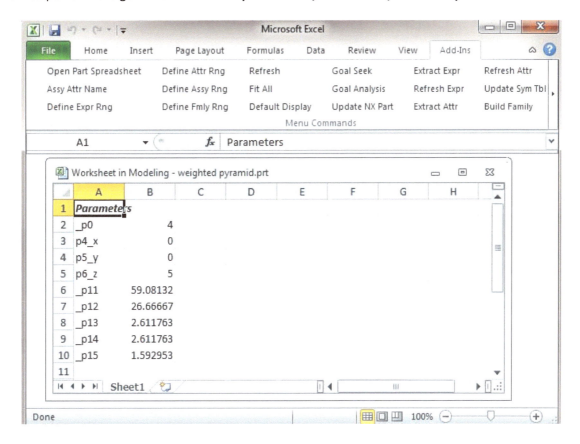

In this case, cell B8 has the mass of the solid.

The goal is to figure out the exact height of the pyramid needed to have a weight of exactly 3 pounds. From the original numbers a 5 inch height yields a 2.6 pound weight, and surely a 20 inch height will yield more than 3 pounds, so let those be the lower and upper brackets.

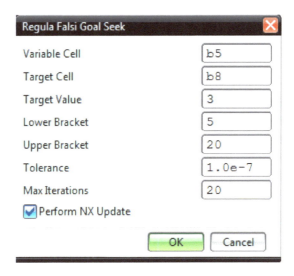

Once the goal seek is run, the result should be 5.74 inches to yield a 3 pound weight.

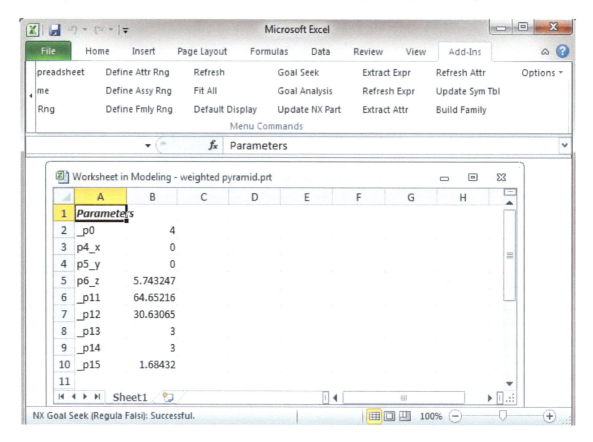

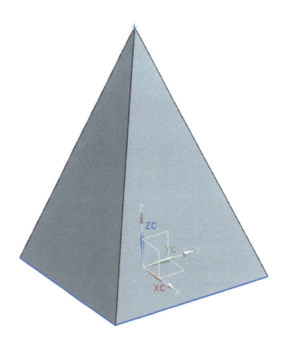

End of Exercise

16. Optimization and Sensitivity

The Optimization function in NX is an amazing way of finding out the answers to difficult design problems by letting NX do the work of iterating certain expressions. If you have a model of an assembly that has geometry of a complex nature and you want to maximize, minimize or find a target value for one of the properties such as surface area, strength, volume etc. the optimization code is a unique and powerful tool. For example, there is a popular calculus problem that many students have studied for decades. It is the one where a farmer has a certain length of fence material and she's going to use it to make a rectangular pen against the wall of her barn. She can make a pen that is long and thin or short and fat. The question is what ratio of length to width does she use to provide the maximum area? In NX you simply emulate the situation with a surface, use a measurement expression to collect the resulting surface area, submit the model to the optimization code with a **maximum** request, and NX will provide the perfect ratio.

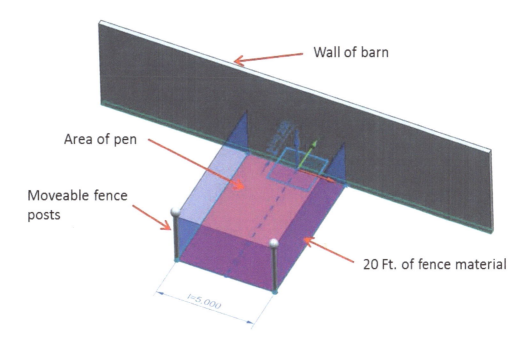

Once the model has been created you access the Optimization code by selecting **Analysis / Optimization and Sensitivity / Optimization.**

The menu that appears requires you to fill in all the various options and run a "**Study**".

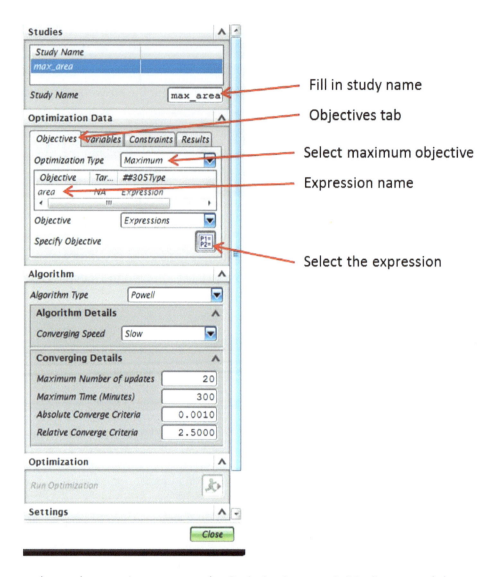

Fill in study name

Objectives tab

Select maximum objective

Expression name

Select the expression

In this case the study name is **max_area**, the Optimization type is **Maximum**, and the expression that is being optimized is the surface area that was assigned to the floor of the pen.

Next you have to select the **variables** tab, select the expression that you will be varying (in this case "**I**"). Also input a value for the lower limit and upper limit. Once you're done select **Run**.

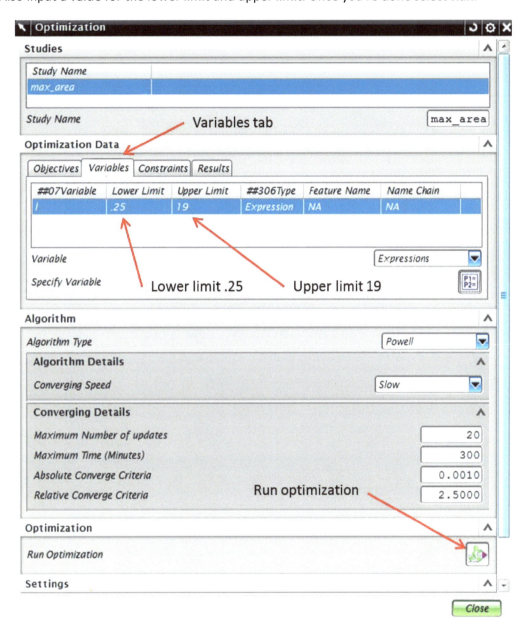

When the case is run, the results will be shown in the "**Results**" tab. In this case the answer that is converged upon is "**l**" equal **10**.

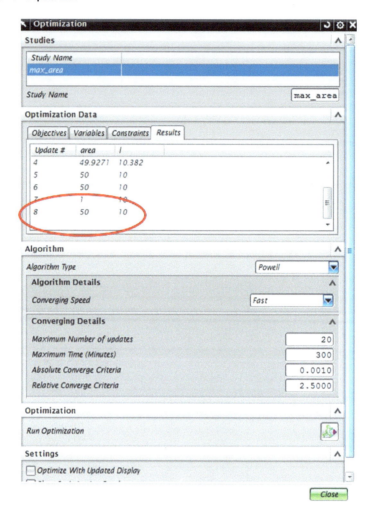

The result appears as shown below:

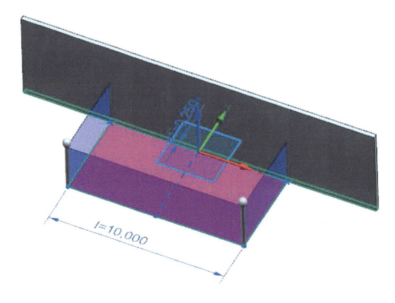

Exercise 16.1 Using Optimization and Sensitivity

One of the really neat things about the optimization ability in NX is that it is capable of considering more than one expression at a time. In this example you will use optimization to search for the perfect location of a tube that will connect two tanks. One tank is spherical on the top and the other is parabolic on the bottom. The centerlines of the two tanks are offset by 7 inches. The diagram below shows the bottom of the parabolic tank and the top of the spherical tank and a line that represents the centerline of the connector. The best connector is the one that is the shortest and the lightest. Using the optimization code NX will iterate the center point distance and the angle of the tube that has the least volume. For this exercise, you may want to retrieve the part file that has already been built (16.1_OptimizationSensitivity.prt) but the following instructions take you through every single step.

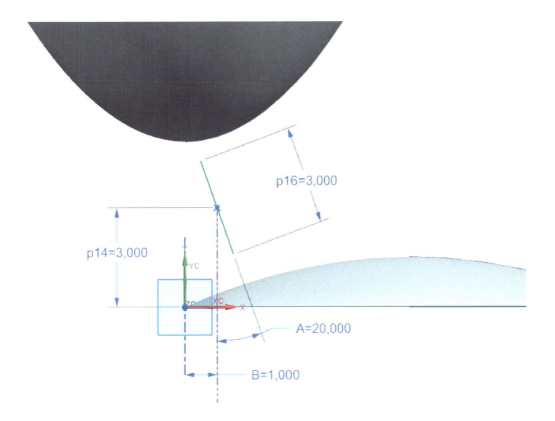

The first step is to create the four expressions that define the law curve for the parabolic tank:

t=1
xt=t*6
yt=5+.15*xt^2
zt=0

Although you may choose other names, choosing the default names xt, yt and zt ensure that the law curve functions creates a curve immediately. Select **Insert / Curve / law Curve.**

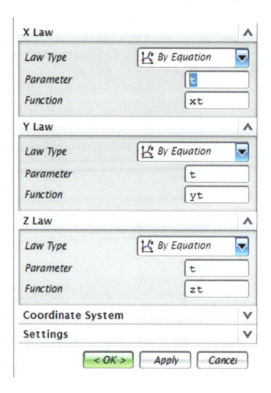

Upon selecting **OK** the formulas that you created for **xt, yt** and **zt** will be accepted and a curve will be created.

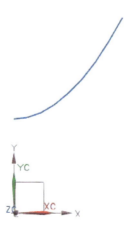

Next create a sketch on the x-y plane with the following dimensions:

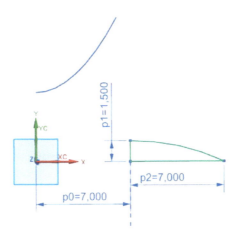

Next create two revolve bodies from the curves. The open law curve is revolved around the Y axis. A revolved open curve will still create a solid as long as the revolve includes 360 degrees.

Next create another sketch on the x-y plane that will represent the center line of the tube that will be used to connect the two tanks. You must rename the horizontal distance dimension to B and the angle to A. Give the expressions arbitrary values of 2 and 25 respectively. Give the line an arbitrary length of 6 inches. Use a point entity to control where the line pivots from.

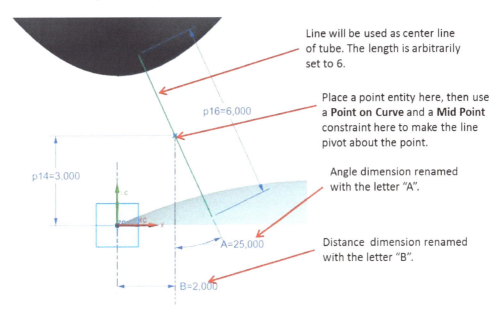

Line will be used as center line of tube. The length is arbitrarily set to 6.

Place a point entity here, then use a **Point on Curve** and a **Mid Point** constraint here to make the line pivot about the point.

Angle dimension renamed with the letter "A".

Distance dimension renamed with the letter "B".

Next, using the angled line and the **Insert / Sweep / Tube** command, create a tube. Input an outer diameter of **1.5** and an inner diameter of **0**.

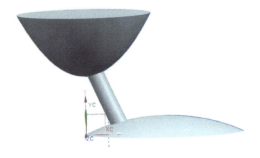

Next, trim the ends of the tube to the surfaces of the bodies of rev. Use **Insert / Synchronous Modeling / Replace Face.**

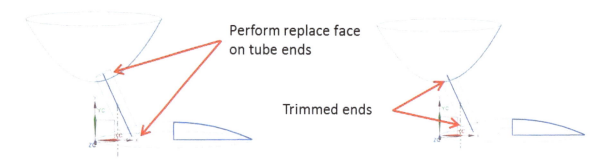

Perform replace face on tube ends

Trimmed ends

Next assign a measurement expression to the resulting body. Use **Tools / Expression / Measurement body.** The expression editor will show a number of expressions. The one that is of concern is the **Volume**. Rename it to "**body_volume**".

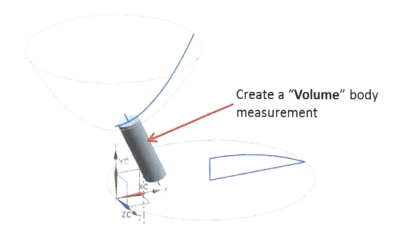

Create a "**Volume**" body measurement

You are now ready to use the **Analysis, Optimization and Sensitivity** ability to find the very lightest tube that can be created. You will ask NX to vary dimension **A** from 0 to 30 degrees and dimension **B** from 1 to 4 inches to find the optimal combination. Select **Analysis / Optimization and Sensitivity / Optimization.** The menu that appears requires certain inputs and selections before the study is complete.

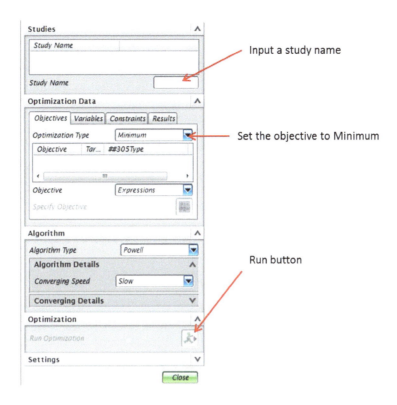

To proceed you must input the name of the study. You may use "**min_v**" and select **OK**. Next specify the optimization type of "**Minimum**". Click on the "**Objective**" tab and make sure it reads "**Expressions**" .

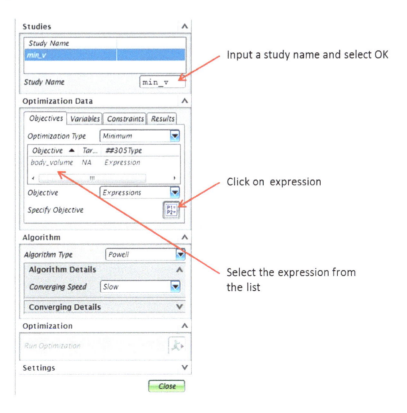

Select the expression "**body_volume**" from the expression pull down.

The next task is to set up the optimization with the correct expressions that will be varied. The tab is labeled "**Variables**". When it comes up you may select the A and B expressions from the list that appears when you select the "**Specify Variable**" button.

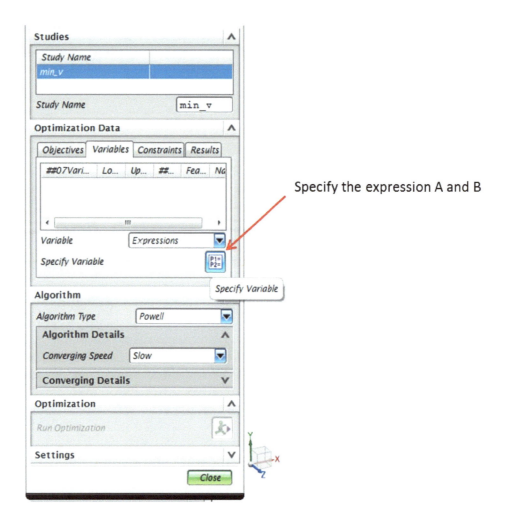

Specify the expression A and B

Once you have entered the expressions **A** and **B**, you must fill in the lower limit and upper limit fields. This is achieved by double clicking into the field locations and inputting values. For **A**, the lower limit is 0 and the upper limit is 30. For **B** the lower limit is 1 and the upper limit is 4.

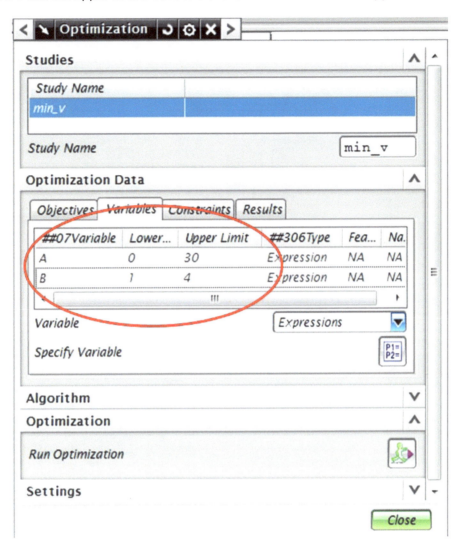

Once you have entered the variables and values, and assuming you are happy with the default algorithm and settings, you my select the "**Run**" button. As NX makes many guesses for A and B combinations you will see the solid update. It will appear to jiggle as it moves into the most optimum angle and distance. The final values will be displayed at the end of the list in the "**Results**" tab. In this example you can see that column 2, the body volume is lowest at 8.14 when the variable A is set to 24.66 and B is set to 1.83.

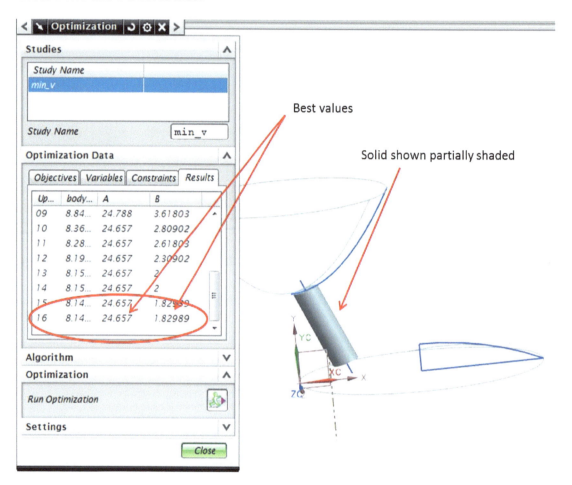

End of exercise

17. What else is amazing about expressions?

If you have gone through many of the chapters of this course you have seen how you can use expressions to do amazing things. You've been given some real world examples and you have hopefully learned a lot. But there's more because an amazing amount of thought has been put into the package. For example, when you have a number of expressions done in a part file and let's say many of them are a function of B; you have XT=3*B, and YT=R*B*cos(t*8*360), etc., when you rename B all the expressions that contained B update to the new name. That's really nice.

Another amazing thing about expressions is the (Functions) button $f(x)$. When you click on the functions button you get the **Insert Functions Menu**, a menu that enables you to see the full catalogue of about 260 functions, search through them all, find out what they do, show you related functions, and even be guided in their use.

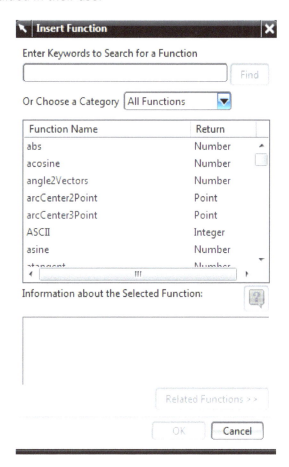

Yet another valuable thing to know about expressions is the fact that with the right set up you can access them from the drafting mode. To do this you need to set the environment variable called UGII_DRAFT_EXPRESSIONS_OK to a value of 1.

Exercise 17.1 Using the Functions Menu

Imagine you wanted to find the force on a member of a certain mass that is holding a rotating body into rotating pattern with a known velocity. Sure you could dig out your physics book, blow off the cob webs and go searching through it, or you could open a metric part file and click on **Tools / Expressions / Functions**:

Next type in "**centri**", short for centrifugal and click on the **Find** command.

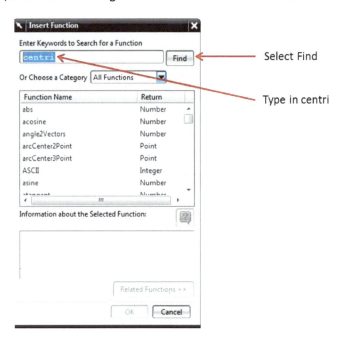

Highlight the **ug_centrifugalForce** function that appears and double click it.

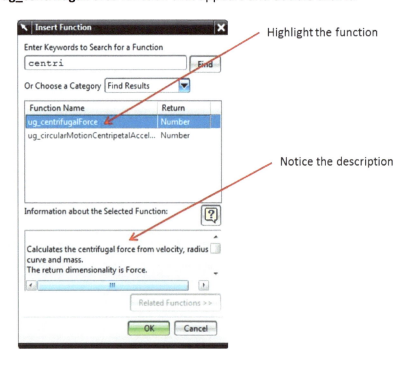

Here's the fun part. Once you've double clicked on the function button a menu appears that allows you to fill in the arguments of the expression that you're creating. For example, let's say you just won a 1975 Chrysler Cordova in a poker game that you had with Ricardo Montalban. It has a classic 70s bench seat.

You're driving down the road with your sweetheart from France in the passenger seat. She's 150 lbs but you know her mass in kilograms (68.75). She weighs 674.4 Newtons on the seat. You notice that she's not yet buckled in. You know that there's a curve coming up that has a radius of about 100 feet (15240)mm. In an effort to impress her you've got NX running on a laptop on the dashboard. There's a new mm part opened and ready. You want to know what's the velocity at which you must travel to have your honey slide into the middle seat, right next to you. Given her friction coefficient upon the rich Corinthian leather is .6, you quickly calculate that you need 674.4× .6 = 404.64 Newtons of force to get her into your out stretched right arm. In a metric part you enter the expressions editor double click on the centrifugal function and get the menu that appears below. You fill in the arguments shown.

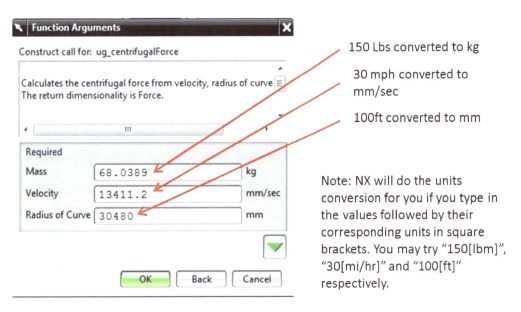

150 Lbs converted to kg

30 mph converted to mm/sec

100ft converted to mm

Note: NX will do the units conversion for you if you type in the values followed by their corresponding units in square brackets. You may try "150[lbm]", "30[mi/hr]" and "100[ft]" respectively.

When you have finished putting in the arguments, select **OK.**

Next, input an expression name; in this example **Force** was used. Don't forget to change the dimensionality to **Force** and change the units to Newtons.

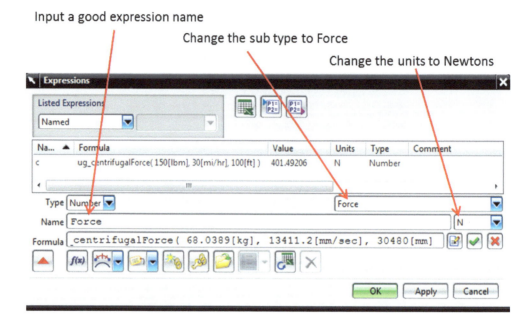

When you select **OK y**ou get a value of 401.49 N. Just enough! Perhaps go a wee bit faster.

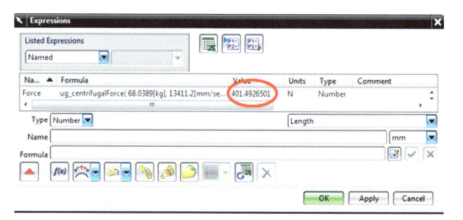

Next try to input the same values with different units in the square brackets.

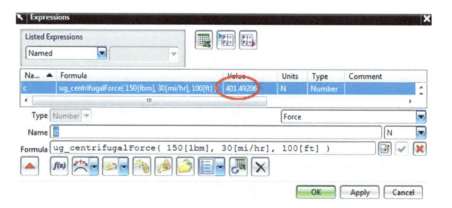

End of exercise

Exercise 17.2 Using the Extended Text Entry Function

The **Extended Text Entry** function (new in NX 8) allows you to semi-automatically build expressions without having to remember the exact required syntax. For example, let us build the expression that says **X=5 if A=10 and B=12, else X=4**.

First we will need to create a new part file and call it what you will.

Next, open the expressions editor and enter the supporting expression in the normal way. **A=10, B=12.**

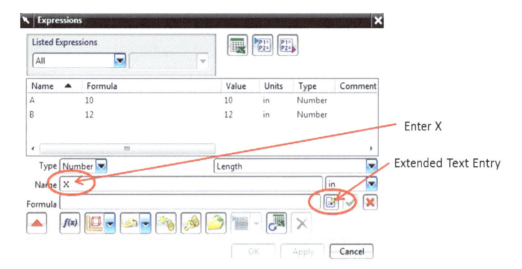

Next, type **X** into the name box, and click on the **Extended Text Entry** button.

Next you will find yourself in the Conditional Builder:

Next enter in the "**if**" box **A=10**, and press the "**&**" button.

Now enter the rest, **B=10.** Enter **5** in the "**Then**" box and **4** where it reads **Else.** Finally select **OK.**

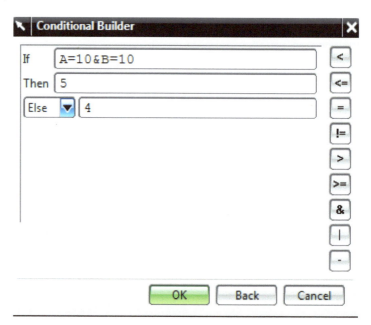

You will see the **Extended Text Entry** confirmation window. Select **OK**.

You will now have a complete new conditional expression. NX will compress your expression formula into one line for display here in the **Expressions Dialog**, but if you return to the **Extended Text Entry** window, your original multi-line formatting will be preserved. The Knowledge Fusion language used for NX expression logic and functions ignores whitespace and line breaks, which gives you great flexibility in laying out complex expression logic in very readable formats, as shown in the conditional expression above.

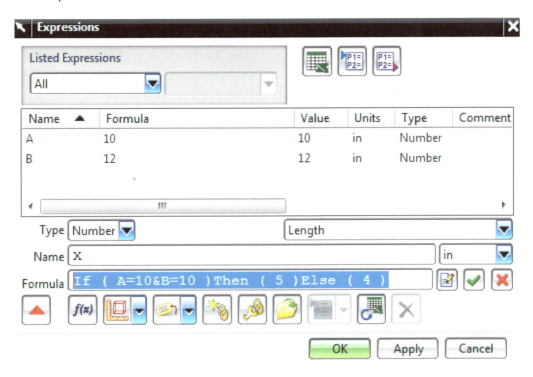

Finally Select **OK.**

End of Exercise

18. Expressions with Part and Object Attributes

Object attributes and part attributes are blocks of information that are attached and associated to a part or to a model object. For example you can have a model of an I-beam with an attribute name associated to the part file called **mfg** that has a value of "**McMaster**". The model may also have a part number, a part description, a surface finish call out, and possibly many other attributes. In NX you have the ability to access the part attributes in the expressions editor. This way you can use the part attributes to place an embossed part number on a part, or import it onto a drawing, etc. This technique works hand in hand with the properties editor. To access the properties editor click on **File / Properties.**

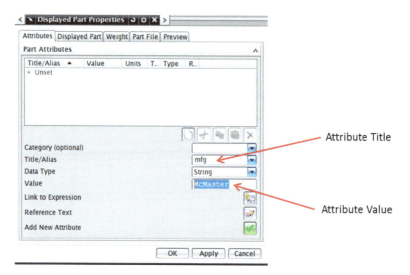

The properties editor allows you to create attribute titles and set values. You access it by selecting **File / Properties.**

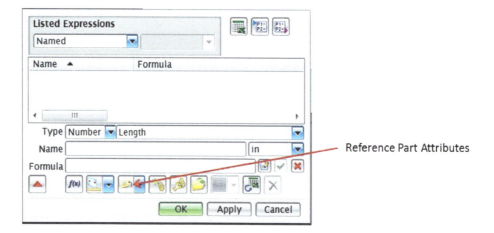

Once you have part attributes, you can proceed to the expressions editor and select on the **Reference Part Attributes** switch. You can make a "**string**" expression that you can use to emboss lettering onto the I-beam. You simply double click on the attribute from which you want to pull a value into your expression.

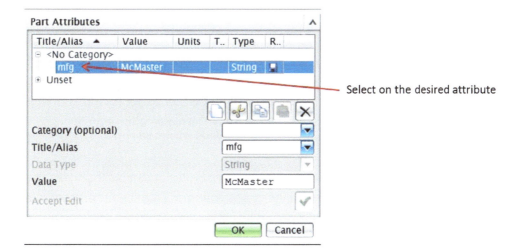

The expression is created and ready for use.

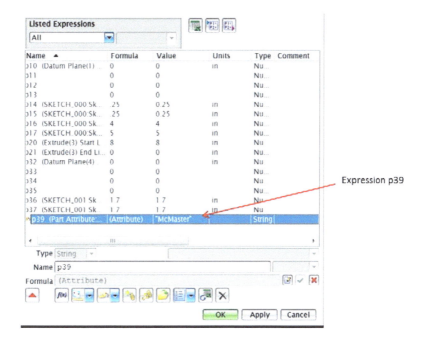

The text command allows the capturing and use of the string expression. When you change the attribute the lettering on the model automatically changes.

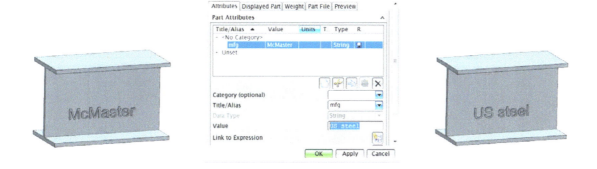

The improvements to the Attributes system (first in NX 8) allow attributes to have datatypes that almost 100% correspond to the datatypes used for expressions. However, the attributes system does not have the ability to perform calculations or perform programmatic formatting. For example, if you have a string attribute VENDOR and a number attribute PART_NUMBER, there's no way (strictly within the attributes system) to combine these two attributes into a third attribute ITEM_CODE that concatenates these two values together into one string with appropriate formatting.

That said, because values can be passed back and forth (attributes can pull from expressions as well) quite easily, the expressions subsystem can be used to perform calculations and operations on attribute values. In the example above, it would be pretty easy to create two new expressions to receive the VENDOR and PART_NUMBER values and combine these into a third expression using the format() function:

...and then pull this value back into a new ITEM_CODE attribute using the **Link to Expression** button back in the Attributes dialog:

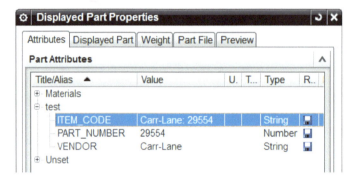

...and as a result of the Attributes work completed in NX 8 (in which changes to attributes can now initiate updates), everything is associative at this point. Changing the VENDOR string attribute will initiate an associative ripple to update the expressions and the ITEM_CODE attribute as well:

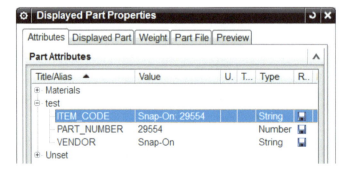

Again, the concept of using the expressions subsystem as a math/calculation/formatting engine for attributes is a new and powerful capability that we didn't have prior to NX 8.

Exercise 18.1 Part Attribute Expressions

In this exercise you will learn how to create a part attribute and assign it to a solid model expressed in text. An application for this technique is when you are creating an electronics housing and you will be modeling actual lettering into the side of it to comply with UL specifications etc. This saves the cost of printed compliance labels that must be specially ordered and printed on special material with special ink - very expensive, ouch!

To begin, create a solid body in a new part file. It can be a block or any other simple solid.

Next create an attribute by selecting **File / Properties** to bring up the menu shown below:

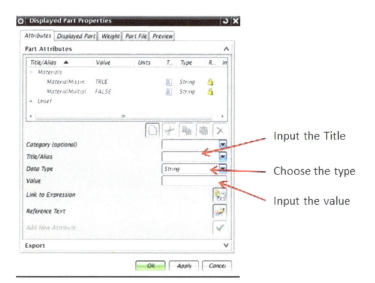

Input "**ul-spec**" into the Title box, make sure the type is set to "**String**" then input "**spec-495**" into the value box. Finish by selecting **OK**.

Once you have created an attribute called **ul-spec**, you can use it to place embossed lettering on the component. Naturally, you may want to update the specification number of the model. With this technique you will not have to remodel the part when you need to make a change, just change the attribute and the lettering will automatically update.

Next, you must create an expression that links to the attribute. Select **Tools / Expression / Reference Part Attribute** 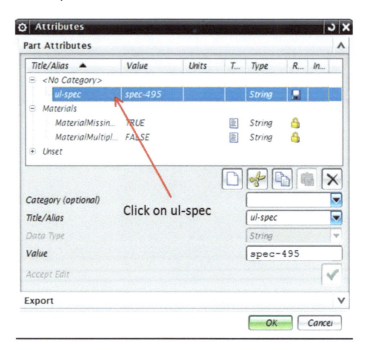. The following menu will appear: Click on the attribute that you created "**ul-spec**" followed by **OK**.

Once you select **OK**, a new expression is created. In this case it is **P6**.

The final step is to use the expression that you created to drive the lettering on the side of the product. First create a line where the text will be drawn.

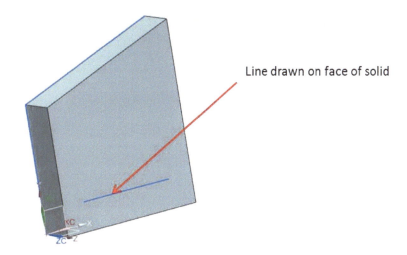

Line drawn on face of solid

Select **Insert / Curve / Text.** Choose the "**On face**" method from the pull down menu and select the face. Then select the line, select the box that says reference text and the box that says expressions.

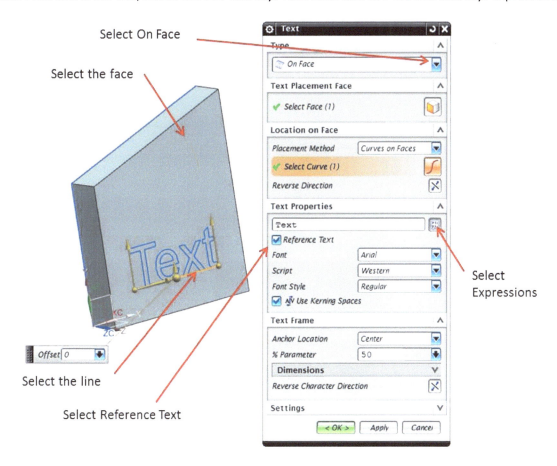

Select On Face

Select the face

Select Expressions

Select the line

Select Reference Text

The **Relationships** dialog will appear with your choice of string variables. For this exercise only the expression that you created will be available.

Once you select on the expression and select **OK** the lettering will appear drawn on the line as shown below:

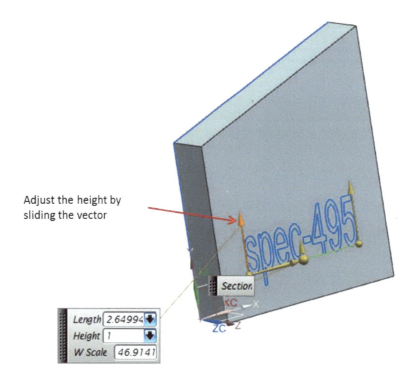

Adjust the height by sliding the vector

To finish the project extrude the lettering. Make sure the selection intent manager reads "**infer curves**". This will ensure that even if you change the lettering so that there will be a different number of characters, everything in the sketch will be extruded. Unite the extrusion and the result will appear as shown below:

Now change the attributes by selecting **File** / **Properties** / and click on the **ul-spec** attribute. Change the value to "**spec-500**".

End of exercise

19. Suppression of Components Using Expressions

NX gives you the ability to suppress and un-suppress components using expressions. The folks who make use of this ability generally have assemblies with a lot of standard parts and a complex suite of products that come in many sizes. For example, the Acme industrial water pump company makes sophisticated pumps for irrigation and such. The machine that irrigates 100 acres is very similar to the one that irrigates 400 acres except it is larger and has an additional pressure control system on it. A simplified BOM for the small machine is; Pipe, Pump, Hatch. The simplified BOM for the larger machine is Larger Pipe, Larger Pump, Larger Hatch, and Pressure Control System. The expression that controls the suppression state of the Pressure Control System lives in the upper level assembly file along with interpart expressions that can control the size of the individual components.

Once you have the ability to make these "smart" assemblies the next thing you might want to know is how to use them to have a more streamlined and efficient business. There are many answers to that question. One simple method is to have a smart master assembly, make the changes that go along with the latest set of requirements, then perform the "**save as**" command. An example is shown below:

In the example we start with an assembly that has everything, the Pump, the Hatch, the Pipe, and the Pressure Control System. The diameter of all the components is controlled via an interpart expression, "**pipe_diameter**" that resides in the upper level assembly part. There is another expression in the upper level assembly file called "**switch**". It controls the suppression state of the Pressure Control System. "**switch**" is actually a conditional statement. If the pipe diameter is greater than 600 mm, the value of the switch goes to 1. If the pipe diameter is less than 600 mm, the value of the switch goes to 0. This turns the suppression state of the Pressure Control System to suppressed. The Pressure control system will no longer show up in the BOM. However, there will be an indication in the Assembly Navigator. The expressions list for the upper level assembly is shown below:

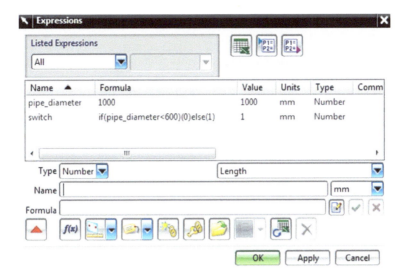

The switch is applied to the Pressure Control System suppression state by performing the following:

The Pressure Control System component is selected in the Assembly Navigator and upon right clicking on **Suppression** the following menu will appear.

Next click on "**Controlled by Expression**" and input the control variable "**switch**" into the box. Once all this is set, the diameter is changed to 500. The assembly changes as shown below. The Pressure control system component appears dashed and blue in the assembly navigation tool.

Diameter changes from 1000mm to 500mm

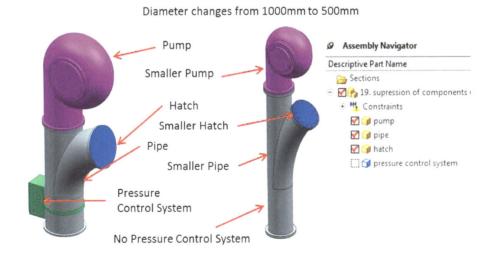

Exercise 19.1 Using Component Suppression Controlled by Expression

In this exercise you will perform a simple suppression of a component in a very simple assembly by an expression that is placed in the assembly part file. To begin create an assembly file called "**Assembly**". Then create two components as shown below. Use any units and any sizes – in this case size doesn't matter. The navigation tool will appear as follows. Notice my naming convention is slightly different.

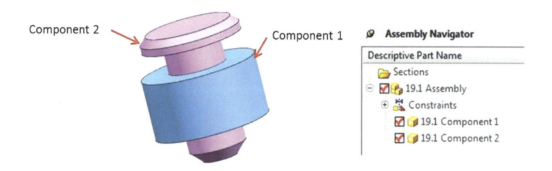

Next, open the expressions editor in the **Assembly** part and create the expression "**switch=0**".

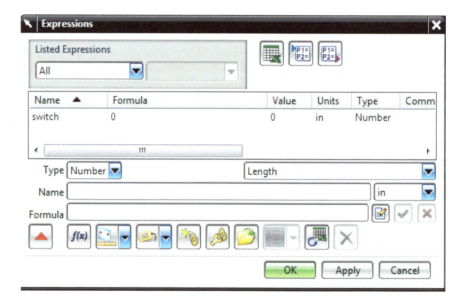

Finally, with the assembly as the work part, left click on **Component 2** in the Assembly Navigator then right click to bring up the menu.

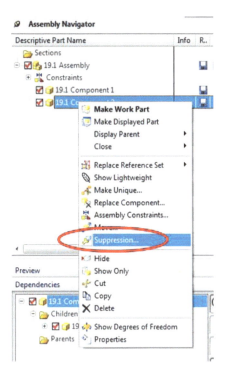

Click on the "**Suppression**" choice in the menu shown above. Then you'll get the **Suppression** menu. Select on the button that reads "**Controlled by Expression**"

Since **switch** equals zero, the assembly will appear as shown below:

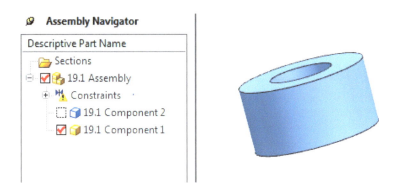

End of exercise

20. Re-Parameterizing Non Parametric Models

We may have saved the best for last. NX is unique in its ability to add parametric data to non-parametric models. Imagine you import a model from a step, Iges or parasolid file. The model you now have is "dumb". At first glance, there's no way to change it parametrically. But the good news is, using many of the synchronous modeling commands, and especially the "**Resize Face**" and "**Dimension**" commands, you are afforded the ability to add parametric expressions to these models. For example, the frame member below was imported from a step file.

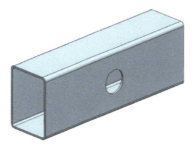

It has no parameters at all. There are no expressions, yet it would be nice if there were some way to control the length with a new expression. Thankfully it's easy with the latest versions of NX. You simply use the synchronous modeling command called **Dimension / Linear Dimension**.

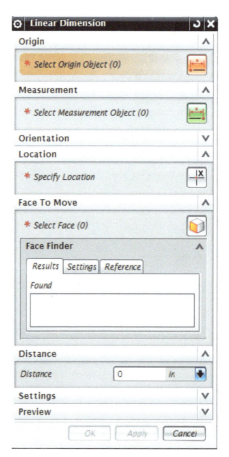

The "**origin object**" can be thou;ght of as the entity you want to "stand still" on one end of the dimension, while the "**measurement object**" will move as the dimension is changed. The system creates a new dimension as shown below:

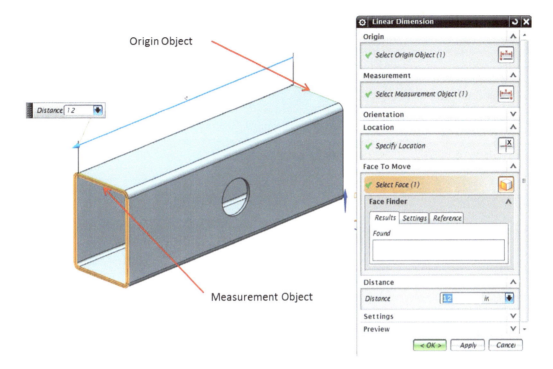

The dimension shows the present value, in this case 12, and allows you to type in a new value. In the background NX creates a new expression that holds the input value. This in turn allows you to change it at will. Essentially you are re-parameterizing the model and making it smart as you go along. As shown below, when the model is given a new linear dimension of "**8**", the left end of the square tubing (the "**Measurement Object**" in the Linear Dimension feature) moves to the right, shortening the part. The right end of the tube stays in the same position, or in more concrete terms, the distance between the hole and the right end of the tube is unchanged.

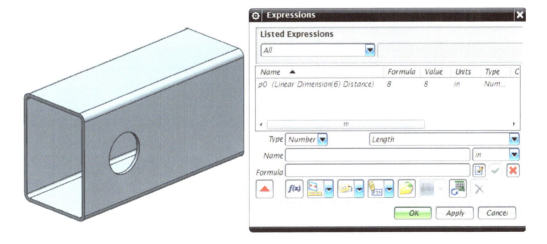

A new **Linear Dimension** feature is created in the Part Navigator, and the dimension expression appears in the expression editor and can be manipulated in the conventional way.

Another dimension that can be easily created is the diameter dimension. Using the "**Resize face**" command, and selecting the interior surface of the hole, a new dimension is created. In the example below a hole that starts out with a diameter of **1.52** is changed to **3**.

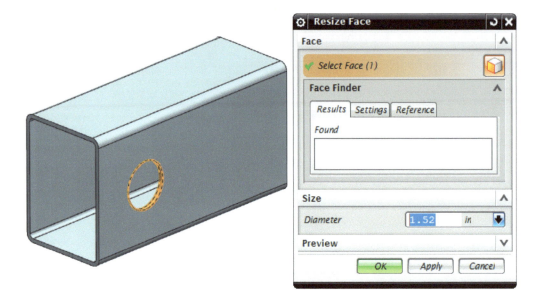

The resulting **Resize Face** feature appears in the Part Navigator and the associated expression appears in the expressions editor as "**p1=3**".

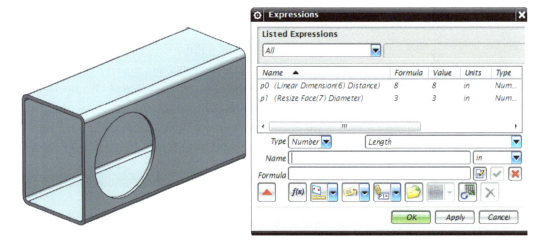

Once **p1** has been created, it can be used in any of the various functions or any other technique that is available for expressions.

Exercise 20.1 The Synchronous Modeling Dimension Command

The **Dimension** command creates a dimension and an expression that controls geometry and adds parametric data to geometry that is either non parametric or parameterized in a way that is no longer advantageous. The same is true for the **Move** command, the **Resize face**, the **Pull face**, **Offset region** and others. To perform an example, begin by creating a block that is **1** by **4** by **10**.

Also blend one corner, 2 inches and add a **1** by **1** boss in the middle.

Now navigate to **Edit / Feature / Remove parameters.** Click on the solid model and click **OK**. The following message will appear:

Upon clicking on "**Yes**", all the prametric data will be removed. Now the model is as dumb as if it had been imported from an iges, parasolid or step file. A lot of engineers at various companies use this command when a model has become too large and takes too long for updates. Notice that the Part Navigator contains only 2 simple entities. Your model is reduced to "**Body**".

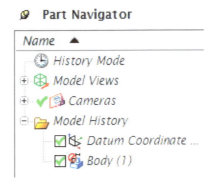

Now the challenge is to place a new set of parametric controls on the model. Navigate to **Insert / Synchronous Modeling / Dimension / Linear dimension.** Select on the bottom edge as shown below, then the top edge and a place to put the dimension. Then enter **15** into the **Distance** box.

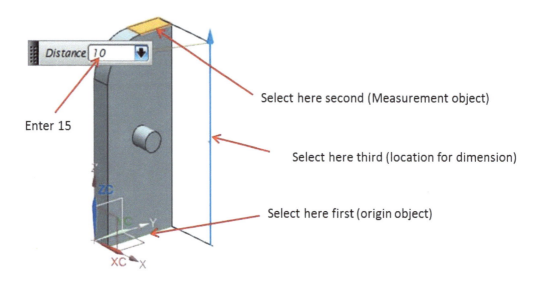

Enter 15

Select here second (Measurement object)

Select here third (location for dimension)

Select here first (origin object)

The result is a taller model with a new parameter / expression set to **15.**

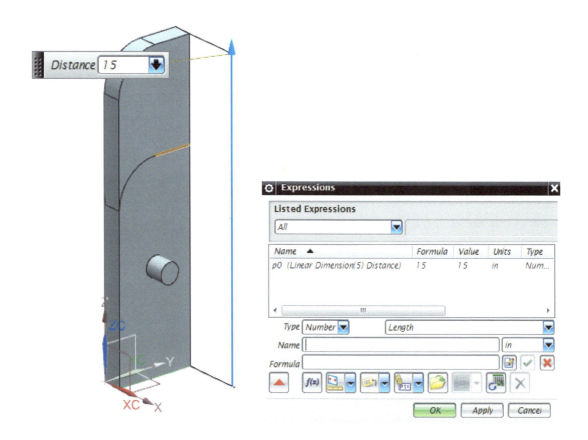

Next let's assume that the intent was to have the boss maintain a middle position as the overall length is varied. Since the length is now controlled by **p0** we need the dimension from the bottom edge of the block to the middle of the boss to be **p0/2**. Navigate back to the dimension command – selecting **F4** (repeat last command) may take you there. Select the bottom edge, then the center of the edge of the boss (you may have to set the selection intent to "circle center" ⊙) then a location for the dimension. Enter **p0/2** and click on **Enter**.

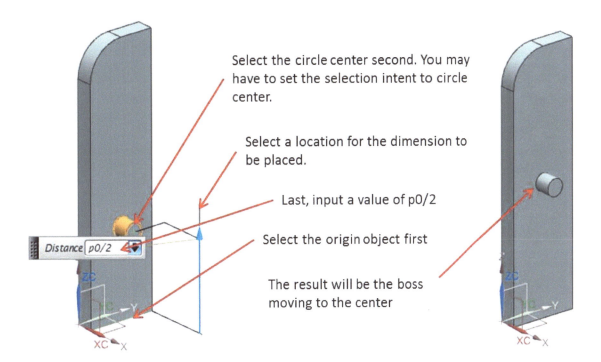

Select the circle center second. You may have to set the selection intent to circle center.

Select a location for the dimension to be placed.

Last, input a value of p0/2

Select the origin object first

The result will be the boss moving to the center

Distance p0/2

End of exercise

INDEX

Other Learning Opportunities (a conversation with the author)

Learning how to create great models and perform real product design in NX is immensely interesting and fun for those who are creative and celebrate the ethic of the product design nerd. For me, a lot of this started when my father used to take my brother and me to the junk yard in the late 60s. In those days the US wasn't nearly as law suit crazy as it is today. You could walk around in a junk yard and pick up all sorts of discarded stuff without anyone worrying that you would sue them if you got hurt. The three of us would delight in taking apart things and get motors, gears and every manner of mechanical component that we would use to try to create other things. Even to this day, I would highly recommend "tear downs". I would highly recommend going to a yard sale and getting very inexpensive products and taking them apart. See how they were put together. Try to get into the head of the designers – try to learn a thing or two. Imagine how the products can be better. Apply what you know to your next project.

For CAD I would highly recommend some of the other books I've penned. They are available at http://designvisionaries.com/books/.

As far as I know, there is no better way to learn CAD then to have an extremely passionate and knowledgeable trainer come to visit. He will take a look at the geometry that you are responsible for and truly focus the training on the techniques that are germane to your specific tasks. He will help you innovate new ways of creating production geometry so that when he's done you will truly be enabled by the experience. You will be extremely well served by this highly motivated guy who's been all over the world and worked with thousands of the most creative and intelligent people. I just happen to know a guy. Give me a call any time. Of course we have a bunch of other types of training too, including on-line and distance learning to fit whatever need you may have.

Once you've been trained, there's a good chance that you will begin to forget the knowledge that you have invested in learning. In order to keep that knowledge fresh we offer a product called **The Sharpener**. Imagine that you or your subordinates could click on a special place within your intranet and receive scores of CAD tips and techniques in video format that were specifically created for your workforce. That is the essence of the Sharpener. If interested please feel free to give me a call.

Stephen M. Samuel, PE   (408) 997 6323

steves@designviz.com